Making Independent Films

Advice from the Filmmakers

Liz Stubbs *&* Richard Rodriguez

ALLWORTH PRESS
NEW YORK

05 04 03 02 01 00   5   4   3   2   1

Published by Allworth Press
An imprint of Allworth Communications, Inc.
10 East 23rd Street, New York, NY 10010

Cover design by Douglas Design Associates, New York, NY

Page composition/typography by Sharp Des!gns, Lansing, MI

ISBN: 1-58115-022-9

LIBRARY OF CONGRESS CATALOGING-IN-PUBLICATION DATA
Stubbs, Liz.
Making independent films: advice from the
filmmakers / Liz Stubbs and Richard Rodriguez.
        p.   cm.
Includes index.
ISBN 1-58115-057-1 (pb)
1. Motion pictures—Production and direction.
2. Independent filmmakers—United States—Interviews.
I. Rodriguez, Richard. II. Title.
PN1995.9.P7 S78 2000
791.43'023—dc21
00-030386

Printed in Canada

We wish to thank all those who had faith in us when our own was running low. And thank you to all the filmmakers who had the courage to stop talking and take the leap.

Table of Contents

Introduction

The Independent Breed

Since the inception of our ability to record and preserve moving images, we have studiously set about to document, abstract, fictionalize, and glorify reality. But throughout the technological metamorphoses modifying the way we physically make movies, one thing has remained constant: their magic. We all, on some occasion, have sat in a darkened theater and been transported to the world on screen. We find personal relevance in select pieces of this world: the humanity and inhumanity of the characters, the swelling strains of the sound track, the poignancy of the dialogue, the rich and exotic hues and images, and the complex texture of the story. Our realities are changed, consciously and unconsciously, because of that connection.

We wish, here, to celebrate what has long been the underdog of the film industry: the independent filmmaker. An "indie," as they are affectionately termed, is defined as one who finances and makes films outside the traditional studio system. But this mercenary definition, though accurate, doesn't fully reflect the indie character. Also by definition, the indie must possess and nurture endless stores of faith, optimism, humor, grit, and perseverance.

You see, independent filmmaking requires fortitude above all else—emotionally, physically, spiritually, and financially. Parents may see it as an unwise career choice. Friends may see it as a hobby, bordering on an obsession. Others may simply nod and remark on how quaintly unconventional you are. Granted, credit card companies may love you, but in a way that you wouldn't prefer.

Choosing to be an indie is cause for second-guessing—especially your own. While your contemporaries are furnishing their four-bedroom homes from the pages of Pottery Barn, you are calling from your rental-sublet trying to wrangle a film crew who will work for meals and not money. While your friends are storing smoked salmon and Starbucks coffee beans in their freezers, you are purveying the stockpile of short ends in yours. When they open a tin of oysters, you reach for the Spam. They contribute to their 401k; you bank on future success.

Ironically, as an indie you lead a life riddled with compromises so you can craft a film without them. You choose this path to ensure that your vision will find life on-screen in its purest form—so that it will not mutate under the pressures of outside puppeteers. You are the choreographer of this dance, but you are also largely its sponsor.

Sound like more of a sacrifice than it's worth? Listen to an indie talk about movies. They speak ardently about films—they watch them, they debate them, they read them, they immortalize them, they support them, they dream about them, they study them, they make them.

Passion. That's the payoff. The visceral, the cerebral, and the sentimental aspirations—they are all sated in the ardent pursuit of filmmaking. Your heart sings, your soul lives—you have contributed an incomparably personal perspective to humanity.

Independent filmmakers are artists. People are their palettes. The screen is their canvas. Story is their frame. And what they paint are possibilities. They ask, "What if?" And by so probing, they prompt us to question the accepted and the unacceptable, the why and the why not, and the what could be. Delicate or indelicate, they don't flinch in their on-screen examination. They don't neutralize and pasteurize and homogenize to achieve the mainstream blend. They are unswervingly loyal to their souls and their voices. And while it may not always be pretty or pastoral, it can be hauntingly and exquisitely beautiful.

Independent filmmakers have in recent years attained vogue status with highly publicized film festivals and Academy nominations. But the celebrity, while good for business, misrepresents independent film in the strictest sense. Many so-called independent films are largely financed by studio dollars. When Miramax backs *The English Patient,* for example, that is not a true independent film.

While directors like John Cassavetes (*Husbands*), John Sayles (*Return of the Secaucus Seven*), Robert Altman (*Nashville*), and Spike Lee (*Do the Right Thing*) had been producing independent films somewhat quietly in the years before 1989, it was Steven Soderbergh who really put independent film in the vocabulary of the mainstream film fan with his directorial debut, *sex, lies, and videotape* (1989).

sex, lies, and videotape was an anomaly in its day. Nevertheless, it's what every first-time indie dreams about in his most honest moments. It was an art film that crossed over to the mainstream audience; it was written and directed by a first-timer; it was made independently on a low budget ($1.2 million); and it generated relatively enormous box office profits (grossing over $24 million in theaters). It opened the floodgates for doubting indies to stop talking and start filming, and it remains the film to which first-timers aspire. It is an indie's beacon of hope, giving credence to what is possible.

The eighties set the scene for independent films to gain a foothold and to begin thriving. Economically, the Reagan Era left baby boomers with disposable cash and the time to spend it on leisure activities. At the same time, the vehicles for movie consumption increased exponentially. The number of movie theater screens increased by about 30 percent between 1980 and 1989; the number of households that subscribed to cable television tripled during the same time period; and by 1989, 75 percent of the households in the United States had at least one VCR—a figure up from only 3 percent in 1980. More people than ever before were buying and renting movies in the eighties. Perhaps more important, however, the baby boomer filmgoers proved to be discriminating viewers and patronized "art-house" films, creating a supportive audience for indie fare.

As far as funding for independent films, it was an easy time to find investors during the eighties. That is, until the stock market crash in 1987. After that sobering event, those with money were less likely to part with it unless they had a reasonable guarantee of return. And with that investment they asked for tighter control over the process and product—provisos that run counter to the very nature of an independent. And because indie films remain largely undercapitalized, their filmmakers have become inventive fund-raisers and marketers by necessity. Robert Rodriguez, for example, rented his body to medical researchers to finance his first feature.

When independent films make money, they get noticed, especially by Hollywood. As with *sex, lies, and videotape,* indie films catapulted into the limelight again in the summer of 1999 with the unprecedented success of *The Blair Witch Project,* an independent feature shot for between $30,000 and $40,000. In less than three weeks after its release, it had earned $35.4 million. And it earned the landmark achievement of highest three-day dollar figure for films opening on at least 800 screens. It averaged over $25,000 per screen that weekend, eclipsing the opening figures for Hollywood blockbusters *Titanic, Jurassic Park,* and *Star Wars: Episode I—The Phantom Menace.* Hollywood may have the bucks, but indies have proven they have the bang.

The filmmakers chronicled in the following pages give voice to the experience of the pure independent. They give you the down and dirty, the nitty-gritty, and the lessons learned. They share their war stories, their insights, their pitfalls, and their triumphs to give every aspiring indie filmmaker a leg up on the ride of a lifetime.

1

Cast of Characters
(in alphabetical order)

Chris Blasingame

A former director of photography from Chicago, Chris shirked a film-school education early on and struck out on his own. Years of writing and shooting culminated in his first short, *Roadrunner* (super-16mm). His short is his entrée to the festival world where he plans to develop a name and reputation on which he can build backing for his next film, a feature. Although film can aspire to the artistic, Chris takes a pragmatic approach to filmmaking, emphasizing that, above all, it is a business, and return on investment is the best way to assure a continuing career.

Roadrunner: A Trailer

Roadrunner is a film about a schizophrenic drifter who pays the price of a small midwestern town looking for a quick, easy answer for justice.

Traci Carroll

With a background in graphic design, Traci brings a strong visual sense to her first short, *Five O'clock Shadow* (16mm). In fact, dialogue is kept to a minimum in this film to purposefully engage the audience. By leaving the visuals open to interpretation, Traci feels films become more personal to viewers, because they must participate in understanding the story instead of being spoon-fed meaning and significance through dialogue. Surprisingly, although *Five O'clock Shadow* was written, directed, and produced by a woman, women's groups have not been entirely supportive of the film because their interpretation seems to be limited to one view. Challenging audiences to flex their interpretive muscle could be her gauntlet as a filmmaker.

Five O'clock Shadow: A Trailer

A man with a razor and a confrontation with the alluring Veronica . . . the film relies on intense visuals to leave the interpretation of the story up to the audience. With only a few words of dialogue, and with no sense of closure to the plot, the film intentionally leaves the audience with just enough information to argue what it was actually about.

Chad Etchison

From the beginning, Chad's world was a stage. He was a stage actor as a child, and his adult pursuits were music and acting. But while working as an extra in television he became intrigued with the job of the director, which to him was a mystery. He set about reading books and magazines and studying films to learn more about that craft. He decided to forego a film school education and immerse himself in a more hands-on schooling. He wrote, directed, produced, and acted in his first film, a feature called *The Initiate* (super-16mm). After his baptism by fire, he realizes that perhaps there was more to learn than he thought, but he is wholeheartedly prepared to do it all again.

The Initiate: A Trailer

The Initiate is a film noir study in obsession. It is a story of evil and its consequences. A small town deputy sheriff uncovers evil, entangles himself in a love triangle, and battles alcoholism and other personal demons while investigating his best friend's death.

Jennifer Farmer

Jennifer Farmer grew up in the world of show business. As a child actress, she learned about the world in front of the lens. But when she moved to Los Angeles, she got much of her behind-the-lens training as a script supervisor. After years of drinking it in and taking classes toward a director's certificate, she felt called to jump into the game. Her first film, *The Incredible Pumpkin Man* (super-16mm), is a short which she helmed from business plan to final edit. Her second film is a feature, *Naturally Native,* which she coproduced and directed with Valerie Red Horse. Both films received critical acclaim at festivals and have cemented in her mind that directing is her calling. But, as Jennifer says, making movies is not simply producing a product. The making of the movie is a sacred process; it's essential that the participants embody respect for the process and collaborate every step of the way. Only then will you find the magic on-screen.

The Incredible Pumpkin Man: A Trailer

A story of magic, mystery, and hope on a dark Halloween night, *Pumpkin Man* is the confluence of a young boy searching for the answers to his parents' divorce, a magical pumpkin, and a mysterious trick-or-treater.

Ali Selim

Ali Selim, a Minneapolis-based writer/director, made his first short in 1993. *Yonnondio,* which was essentially a long music video, received international acclaim, but Hollywood told him to come back when he did a film with actors moving their lips.

His second short film, *Emperor of the Air* (35mm), does indeed feature actors with dialogue and has done well on the festival circuit. His true love is telling stories, but his experience as a commercial director and as an indie has taught him that he must have free reign in that realm. He would rather not tell his stories than have someone dictate how they should be told.

Emperor of the Air: A Trailer

An elderly high school biology and astronomy teacher, who has lived in the same house all of his life, finds himself under a night sky in his front yard, about to perform desperate and outrageous acts to ensure the safety of an ancient but diseased elm tree that he used to climb as a boy. The conflict he is having with his neighbor over the sick tree causes the old man to look to the stars in an attempt to unroll and make sense of the navigational charts of his life.

Michael Shoob

After graduating from Wesleyan University with a degree in English, Michael Shoob dabbled in various jobs—bartender, liquor store clerk, waiter, house mover, and cabdriver—where he consciously and unconsciously absorbed slices of life. During this restless period, he also penned *Parasite,* the 3-D horror movie that boasts Demi Moore's screen debut. But it was his stint as a cabdriver that provided the fodder for *Driven* (35mm), his first feature as a director. *Driven* garnered much acclaim and attention at festivals and has earned Michael a solid foundation in the independent world.

Driven: A Trailer

Three renegade and road-weary cabdrivers are eking out a living on the streets of Los Angeles for a second-rate cab company. With the New Year coming and the grim possibility that they will never escape a life of failure, these cabdrivers yearn for some way to be "somebody" in a world that believes they are "nobodies." They find inspiration in the appearance of a cabbie with a seemingly mystical presence.

David Zeiger

Artistically, David's roots are in still photography. But in the course of working on a documentary exhibit, he realized that still photography wasn't enough anymore. He wanted to hear voices; his subject needed more than pictures to adequately tell the story. So, teamed with a filmmaker friend, David shot and edited his first documentary, *Displaced in the New South* (16mm and Hi-8 video). His first effort won acclaim from important corners in the documentary world and encouraged him to shoot his second, more personal documentary, *The Band.* David professes his strengths to be in documentaries, but for his next project, he is crossing over to narrative film and is writing the script for a feature based on *The Band.*

The Band: A Trailer

The Band is the story of a trip the filmmaker took into his son's world. When his son Danny was seventeen and a junior in high school, Zeiger realized suddenly that Danny's life as a kid was rapidly ending. He wanted to capture that moment in time and see the world through his son's eyes. In the context of the high school marching band, he filmed Danny and his cohorts as they made their way through another school year. The film deals with both father and son's struggles to live with the death of Danny's brother several years earlier; Danny's first painful love with Mary Ellen, a girl in the grips of anorexia; and all of the students' wit, intelligence, and wisdom as they maneuver their way through a world filled with complex race relations, divorce, and the prescription-drug culture of the nineties. A film about "life, love, and marching in formation," *The Band* is a coming of age story of both son and father.

2

Training and Inspiration— The Birth of a Career

Clearly, film school was not a panacea for these independent spirits. Those who did choose to begin film school all felt it could not fulfill their needs as much as jumping into the fire and making their own films. Education, for them, came largely via books, life experiences, and on-set osmosis.

They come from varied backgrounds: acting, still photography, graphic design, screenwriting, script supervising, and commercial directing. Some chose shorts for their baptismal experience, others plunged into features. Some authored their scripts; others adapted them from existing works. Some chose narrative form to tell their stories; another lensed reality with a documentarian's eye.

All of them agree that it is precisely their disparate backgrounds and rich life experiences unrelated to film that enhance what they bring to the table as directors. And, no less important, they all have a passion they are unable to quench except through film.

Michael Shoob

My degree from Wesleyan University is a B.A. in English. And you could probably say that I did graduate work at the American Film Institute (AFI) where I was a directing fellow.

My feeling is that there are a thousand routes to making films. Folks come to Hollywood and become writers, editors, and production designers and then get a chance to direct or produce. There's no right way.

I lived in a van with a partner when I first hit town, and we wrote our first screenplay while house-sitting and living in the van. My belief is that you should put time in on all fronts—working on films, making small films yourself, writing, and doing as many jobs unrelated to film as you can to learn a little about life that isn't movie life.

For me, film school was a mixed experience. I had been a screenwriter for a significant amount of time going in. So, it was a great opportunity for me to test my impulses by having to make these films myself. I learned a lot about what works on the page versus what is going to work on the screen. The strongest argument for film school is that it forces you to go out and make the projects and see how you do. I also made some great friendships with other filmmakers that have lasted to this day.

On the other hand, I thought the level of instruction (at the time) and the inevitable political maneuvering often kept the experience from being as terrific as it might have been. In fact, I just went to a screening this week by a recent film school grad and he took me aside and whispered, "Wait until I tell you about the politics I had to face." So I suppose politics and the maneuvering I describe is just part of any film program where there are a lot of very hungry and ambitious young filmmakers. It's probably no different at film school than in the working film world.

On balance, I would probably recommend the film school experience. You get an opportunity to test your ideas, meet a lot of folks who are going to be in the industry with you for a long time, and have your thinking challenged by faculty and other filmmakers.

I think it's fair to say that I wanted to make an independent film for a long time. I had one terrible misfire: I took a terrific cast to a beautiful Appalachian location, and the film died two days from day one of principal photography. After that experience it took a litany of false starts to get another shot at a film. I partnered with some producers. A project was written. Funding was raised. Another project was written to replace project one. More funding was raised. The partnership more or less fell apart while funding sort of teetered in place. I decided to try to write yet a third film, this time more deeply personal. Then, one displacing earthquake and a divorce later, I found my way into the script for *Driven*. I was doubting whether we had the financial resources to make the film, but Bob Logan said to me, "Go ahead and give yourself a green light." So we went ahead and pulled together a team of people who were dedicated to the film. (It turned out I was right about the money, and we had to raise more during and after production.)

What is the film about? Actually, Todd McCarthy, in his *Variety* review, was very helpful in this regard. He described *Driven* as a ". . . fable about not making it in the American rat race." That's one of the best descriptions of what the film is about that I've heard. My usually feeble response is that the film is about a bunch of cabdrivers in L.A., or it's *Glengarry Glen Ross* in a cab. I introduced the film at the second Toronto screening with a hopefully unpretentious quote from Yeats: "In dreams begin responsibilities." I think that is a window on what this cabdriving film should be talking about.

Before I wrote the script for *Driven* I was a cabdriver. I didn't set out to be a cabdriver. I literally was broke, and it was a job I fell into. I ended up doing two separate tours of duty, which amounted to more than a year. It's a job that truly has, as the cliché goes, a million stories. In fact, you are privy to at least a dozen vignettes a day, and if you are fascinated by people and lives which can dramatically crisscross economic lines in the space of five minutes, you can't help but see the story possibilities. I kept a journal for at least part of the time, sometimes even pulling over and writing or transcribing feverishly between fares.

I was especially fascinated by some of the guys I became friendly with.

They seemed, in so many cases, to be marginalized by life. Why would a guy who had been to law school never practice, but prefer to drive a cab? Why would another guy keep trying to create little businesses but never seem to get ahead? Why would another guy seem never to fit into a conventional life—even though he had what seemed to be all the right stuff to succeed?

I was interested in these guys. I wanted to vindicate the nobodies who are wallpaper to most people. I wanted the nobodies to become somebodies by the end of the picture. So that became a theme, and it also became a bit of a mission.

I was also fascinated by the cab as a moving window on the world. It was voyeuristic. It was dangerous. An unmitigated experience of the streets. And frankly, I had never seen the life of cabdrivers accurately portrayed. I felt that Scorsese's film was really about a loner or a psychopath. I didn't feel that either Scorsese or Schrader, who wrote the script, were really out to capture the cabdriving life. I thought Jim Jarmusch's *Night on Earth* used cabdriving as a kind of conceit. So, with the exception of Rob Nilsson's *Signal 7,* which I've never seen, I felt that the cabdriving life was basically virgin territory.

Of course, I worried quite a bit that folks would say to themselves, "Who wants to see a film about cabdrivers?" And this fear both animated and haunted the writing process. I worried about it up to the final moment I actually gave someone the script to read. But it also made the film a mission. I felt that this was a story I was particularly suited to tell. It was something very personal to me.

In the writing, I felt that I was developing something more deeply personal than I had written before. Also, I had been determined to make an independent feature for a number of years. These two skeins were moving concurrently and, ultimately, were on a collision course. I had to make this film NOW! This was going to be the script, and I was going to die trying to make it work. When my "kitchen cabinet" of people seemed to feel that the script was something special, something worth making, I think that redoubled my feeling that this project was the one.

10

Michael Shoob directs Tony Todd as Darius Pelton.

An important point is, I think, that when one sets out to make an independent film, it helps everybody from the production designer to the actors if it's something you know and are passionate about. I rarely had to argue with an actor about the lives I had created, though Chad Lowe and I disagreed on the pronunciation of the word "variegated." He got his way, and the line worked fine.

Also, in evaluating a project to do as an independent film, I realized that I would be living with this thing for a very long time—through the writing obviously, but also through what you might call pre-preproduction before much of the team was in place, through preproduction, production, a long post, and many months of marketing and festival play. And one has to do so many thankless things in the course of this process. I felt in the beginning, and I certainly feel stronger about it even now, that your project better be something that, as a filmmaker, you believe in.

How do you know if a project is right for you? It's probably a combination of your instincts about the project and your readiness to walk

Jennifer Wynne Farmer and her seven-year-old son, Austin (as young Jason in the dream sequence), on the set of *Pumpkin Man*, April 1997. © Pumpkin Pictures LLC.

through the door. Maybe it's that you're ready to believe, and you're ready to try.

Jennifer Farmer

I grew up in show business. My mother had a television show in the Washington, D.C. area, and I did acting as a child in commercials. My stepfather had an advertising agency, so I went on to produce and direct some local car-dealer ads for him. Then I went to North Texas State University and majored in music/music education. I got a degree from Stephens College in Columbia, Missouri, in radio/TV/film. So I had that kind of training as well as life experience.

When I moved to L.A., I got involved in different film companies doing different things, but I became a script supervisor predominantly. I was a script supervisor for eight years, which gave me an incredible amount of on-the-job training in film and TV. I did shows such as *Beverly Hills 90210,* and I did a few days on movies like *Poetic Justice.* I did second unit on *Nothing to Lose.* I did the entire *Last Chance* detective series, which the Paxson Network has recently bought for Focus on the Family. As a script supervisor, I was in charge of maintaining continuity, taking all the notes for the editor, being the right hand for the director, doing shot lists and coverage, and things like that. The experience really gave me good exposure and taught me a little bit about directing and how to approach it.

I had many mentors. Most of the directors I worked with as a script supervisor were either willingly or unknowingly mentors to me. Bob Garner certainly was one of the main ones. Michael Jacobs, who is a producer with Disney, was very kind to me. Just about every director I worked with gave me good advice or set good examples of what to do and what not to do.

And when you work with enough first-time directors, you say to yourself, "You know what? I know I can do this." I literally felt called to do this. I had been teaching script supervising at the Director's Film Lab at the Robert Redford Institute in 1993 and 1994. So I was coming into the game pretty well educated. I was also getting my director's certificate from the UCLA extension program. I was about one-half to three-fourths of the way through that program when I decided to jump into the pool myself.

I found a script, actually a short story, that had been written by a very dear friend of mine named Bob Garner, who is head of the film and TV department at Focus on the Family. The story was called *The Incredible Pumpkin Man,* and it had been printed in the *Saturday Evening Post* seven years in a row. I knew it to be a wonderful family story. But Bob did not have time to write the screenplay for it, so I went to my friend Dino Andrade. His wife is the voice of Snow White for the Walt Disney Company, and my husband is the voice of Goofy and Pluto for the Walt

Disney Company. So Dino and I had become friends hanging out while our spouses would do their work. I know that Dino is a great writer—particularly of the horror genre—so when I was looking to do a Halloween film, I thought of him. I knew that by putting this very sweet story—which was probably too sweet to be a good movie—in the hands of a horror writer that yellow and blue would make green. I handed the story to Dino, and I said, "Now I want this to be a family film with a nice kind of warm fuzzy ending. And I'm much too much of a girl to direct anything icky." He was sort of chagrined when he left, but he came back with a brilliant forty-four-page script.

Ali Selim

I did not attend film school. Living in Saint Paul, Minnesota, the options for film schools were few and far between. However, if I had the opportunity, I don't think I would have chosen film school. I studied English, philosophy, and theology at a small liberal arts college and learned to think and write critically—a skill that I have since learned is the one thing that gets me through most filmmaking obstacles. The technical aspects of filmmaking can be taught in a matter of days or even hours. The thing, the *je ne sais pas quoi,* that makes a film great is not teachable. If one has it (and precious few do), I believe that a film school can bring it out, but it cannot put it where it wasn't. So I am glad I did not have the choice to go to film school. I am happy with where I am today and where I am going, and I don't think I would be anywhere near here had I interrupted my development to go somewhere and study film.

I am still learning my job. There are many times when I feel I couldn't teach filmmaking at all. And then there are other times when I feel I could teach it to anyone. I do read some books on the subject and have obviously learned while doing, but I feel my job is more about knowing the rhythms of humor and drama and knowing how to communicate them clearly and simply to an actor and a cameraman. The books for that are rare. I like David Mamet's *On Directing Film,* and I get a lot from the interviews in *Creative Screenwriting* magazine. Hands-on experience for me is limited to those moments when an actor really gets what I just said or, more often, really doesn't.

I have no mentor. Directors are notoriously egocentric, and for one of them to take another under his or her wing would really be like Ka helping Mowgli survive the jungle. The "What's in it for me?" mentality can get in the way of mentoring. I did become friends with an ad agency creative director who was very supportive and taught me a great deal about people and about clear communication. He is not a filmmaker, and I learned nothing from him about lenses or crossing the line, but I do see his influence in nearly everything I create.

In 1993, I made *Yonnondio*, a short—it is really a long music video—which did very well on the festival circuit. *Yonnondio* won several awards, and I was flown to London, Spain, and Tokyo to talk about it. It won a Cine Golden Eagle from the International Conference on Non-Theatrical Events. The nice thing about this award is that it landed me a distributor, Media Inc., which is still selling the film. I still get small checks, but more importantly the film is being shown.

Yonnondio also won a Silver Award from the Chicago International Festival. But the best experience for me was its inclusion in the London International Film Festival and its being selected for competition in the Bilbao Festival in Spain. Both were great learning experiences—chances to meet other filmmakers and see other films.

Yonnondio is fifteen minutes long—made with a spring-wound Bolex for around $9,000. A song written by a friend of mine inspired it. His small, New Age record label put up most of the money. Everything except gas, processing, and tape stock was donated. I sent *Yonnondio* to several Hollywood agents in the hopes of finding representation. All of them said, "Nice. Call me when you do something with actors moving their lips."

Rather than be dejected by Hollywood's reaction to *Yonnondio*, I was inspired.

Traci Carroll

I was definitely self-educated. My dad was one of those people who assumed I was definitely going to college, and I was definitely going to University of Georgia because that's where he went. I had always been good at art, so my dad sent me this article about graphic design and said, "This is what you should do—you would be very good at this." There was no film school up there—only a journalism major for radio/TV/film, but graphic design was what my dad saw as a reasonable career. Filmmaking would have been a really hard sell. So I went ahead and got a degree in graphic design and another degree in art education, so I would have teaching to fall back on. But I'd always been really interested in film.

The graphic design major has probably been to my benefit because I've ended up being in a situation where I probably make more money than I would had I gone into some filmmaking job when I graduated. I know a lot of people who are really struggling as production assistants or camera assistants or whatever, and they work so hard and so many long hours that they don't have time for their own projects. What I've found is that the job I have is really nine to five, and after that I have my weekends and my nights to work on my projects.

I took the job that I have now thinking I would go back to school and get some sort of master's degree in film. And the guy I was dating at the time said, "Why are you going to spend $50,000 on school when you can make your own film for less than that?" I thought, "Wow I never thought about it like that." He convinced me that, not only would I be able to make a better film, but that I would learn more because I would really be dealing with the vendors and whatever. So suddenly it became this possible thing that I could make my own film rather than having to go back to school. So I didn't go back to school. The only thing is if you go to a good film school like NYU or AFI you do have all of those connections, and with a phone call you can get yourself in somewhere doing something. As a true independent who didn't go to school, I don't have that luxury.

After I first got my job where I am now I heard about IMAGE Film and Video Center of Atlanta, a nonprofit media arts center. So I got on their mailing list and started getting fliers about the classes they offered. I took a history of independent film class, the cinematography class, and two of their scriptwriting classes. I felt like IMAGE was really the place where I could pursue filmmaking, and I could really learn how to do it without having to go to a university and having to pay the expense of being in university filmmaking classes.

I've gotten to see a lot of student films, and the problem with student films is that the university doesn't have the top-notch equipment. You have to struggle to get time with the equipment along with all the other students making films. And particularly, the lighting equipment is more geared for shooting in a specific situation that the university might have set up or for shooting with available light outside. At IMAGE, we were working with a professional DP (director of photography) who knew what he was doing and knew what he wanted to use and had the connections at the equipment houses. He was able to say, "This is what I need, and I would like a really good discount on it." We actually ended up with a film that looks much more professional than any student film I've seen.

Brian Turner and I met in design school. He knew I was taking the IMAGE classes and he said, "Hey you and I should make a film together." And it was a lot less scary to think of doing it with someone else instead of going solo—so if we failed, we failed together, and if we succeeded, we succeeded together.

David Zeiger

My artistic background is in still photography. I was an aspiring writer in high school, but I took a detour in the sixties and got real involved in the antiwar movement and the radical movement, and I stayed with that for a long time. That stage of my life fell apart at the same time that my first marriage fell apart. My whole world had deteriorated. It was then that I picked up the camera. It was ironic; the reason I picked up the camera and started shooting was because I realized all the pictures I had of my kids, Michael and Danny, were taken by my father. I wanted to see what kind of pictures I would take of them. So I started taking pictures of them. It was one of those things where my life was at the bottom of a pit, but I started doing this and there was this revelation—I had this emotional attachment to it and a response to it that I hadn't felt for anything in years. So that was obvious to me—to start in pictures. So that's what I did. I worked as a typesetter and I went to school—that's when I was in Michigan. I took a lot of photography courses, and when I came back down to Atlanta after Michael died I started working in theater companies. I'd had a girlfriend in Ann Arbor who was an actor, and I would shoot at the theater group that she worked with. That became my specialty, so that's what I continued when I got here. Then I went into documentary photography.

Displaced in the New South began as a photography exhibit. As a photographer I spent two years shooting it. We worked for a couple years and put together this exhibit that did pretty well, but that's when I realized that photography wasn't doing it for me. I wanted to hear voices. I felt like there was so much more that could be done about the subject, about the issue, about these people, that I just wasn't able to do with photography. That's when I had contact with Eric Mofford. I had known Eric for a while because I had seen his film *Travelin' Trains* and had liked it a lot, and we became friends. I told him, "I want to make this film. Will you help me make it?" And he said, "Sure."

Filmmaking—I've learned it by the seat of my pants, literally as I've been doing it. I've learned that one of the best things you can do when making a film is hire or get around people who know what they're doing technically and who you can be in sync with artistically. That's pretty much how I've learned—as I've done. I don't have time to go to film school—I can't do it. And sometimes I feel like, "Damn, I'm starting so late. I'm way behind." But then I figure I've lived a lot, I've seen a lot, and I've got a lot that I'm bringing to the table here. So I'm kind of starting out. But if I had started making films when I was twenty, I don't know if I would have developed as a good filmmaker. If I'd done it then, it certainly wouldn't have been very good.

18

Chris Blasingame

I did go to film school. I did not finish film school. I just always felt it was sort of—and not to offend anybody who has degrees—a useless degree. I always thought it was a useless degree unless you're going for the history of it and then it's a valid degree. I always thought the best filmmakers came out of different walks of life and found filmmaking as a second career.

I did filmmaking in high school. I was in the theater in high school and they needed some multimedia, so I did some films and that was my start. They chose me because I did photography so I knew a little bit about it. And then I saw *Eraserhead* (David Lynch) and that did it for me. I decided I was going to get into film.

I went to Hampshire College in Amherst, Massachusetts, which focused on the art of film. At the time in the mid-1980s they had three eight-plate flatbeds that I drooled over. But nobody could tell me how to take a light reading there. So then I went to Columbia in Chicago which was all technical and was glorified high school. They had so many students there that they didn't even teach you how to do sync sound until the third year. I was fed up with it all. So I went to a local rental house and said, "OK, show me how to use this stuff," and they showed me. I made a sync sound film my first year out of Columbia, and I decided, "Why spend my money on tuition?" In retrospect I wish I had the patience to go through a program, but I did not have the patience to go through any of these programs. They were too slow—way too slow.

I won money in 1989 right after I left college, and I started buying equipment. I won't tell anybody that buying equipment is a stupid idea, but it can be a waste of money unless you're buying the best and it's not going to become obsolete down the road, and unless you're using it all the time—which I don't do. But I don't regret doing it because I started making films instead of waiting for Columbia to tell me when I was able to do a sound film. I didn't want to wait. I had a real bad experience with equipment in film school—people screwing it up and that kind of thing. I don't think you learn much by planning a production and finding out

19

your camera's not there because somebody else took it out behind your back. In college, we were on a seniority list, and whoever was there longest had final call on the equipment. So I had fifteen people going to Cape Cod to shoot this one film. I had everything planned. The night before, this person who outranked me decided that she wanted my camera, so she took it and didn't even use it that weekend. So I wasn't going to pay tuition for that crap. There's no sense of community—no sense of We're all in the same boat, so let's help each other out.

I worked with Andy and Larry Wachowski a little bit. They are the writers/directors of *Bound* (1996) and *Matrix* (1999). My sister had met Andy, and he did film. I guess 1985 through 1988 were the college years and then 1989 through 1991 were the Andy and Larry years. And when it was looking like I was going to be the DP on bigger projects for them, I went to the Workshops (the International Film and Television Workshops in Rockport, Maine) to get used to 35mm and to know all those cameras—that was 1992.

Working with Andy and Larry, we didn't go out and shoot a million feet of film. Larry wrote a film—I'm not sure if it was Larry and Andy—called *Night*. It was a short eleven-minute film. And we did that in 1990 or 1991. I think 1991. And that's all we did. We never shot film—we only shot it that one time—we always talked about it. The good thing was that they had a plan, but it was very frustrating that we never shot any more film like I thought we should. Larry went to New York and conceived *Carnivore*, which was the first thing that got them attention. I think I sat in on that but then there was a brother dynamic between the two of them, and I wasn't even a brother—I was very low on the totem pole.

I wanted to be a DP. I think there's no more pure occupation in film, besides the editor, that makes filming unique than the DP. So I was really gung ho about being a DP. At the same time we weren't shooting a lot. I was typing and editing their scripts while we were waiting. So that was what I did because we never shot anything—actually we did shoot the promo trailer for *Bound*—but it was mostly working on scripts at that point.

Since film school I've always been writing, but I'm not a writer so I've never gotten anything done until I forced myself to. I've always wanted to write because I wanted to make my own ideas, but with Andy and Larry I wasn't writing. I was writing on the side for myself.

I've done short films, but *Roadrunner* is the first thing I've done with any production value. I've done about four shorts as a director—they were about eleven-minute college-type things—two in college and two between 1989 and 1995. Directing was always my intention, but I was always doing other things like Steadicam and AC-ing (assistant cameraman) and stuff because I thought I had to do more of that. And then I just got fed up working on other people's projects. I think there was a string of films that either never happened or fell apart midway because of bad conception, bad management, and a script that was out of control. I decided, "Well I'm not working this industry anymore unless I'm doing it for myself." And I'm fine with that. I think I'd rather work at McDonald's than just work on other people's films. And I would gladly help anybody who came my way, which is the weird thing, but I don't want to plan on making an independent living making other people's films. It's frustrating.

Chad Etchison

I never went to film school. I thought about it a little bit. I took a 16mm class taught by Atlanta DP Jim Hunter. It was a great class—I learned to use the camera, to load the mags, and to shoot film. I shot some film, but it was really pitiful. I shot the footage and then I put it on the Steenbeck, and it looked terrible. I got it in focus but I was using a zoom lens, and I didn't understand how to use grad filters and didn't really have a good grasp of cinematography at all. I knew how to load the camera and shoot something, but that's it. I didn't understand the art of operating or any of that. That's what made me decide that I was definitely not going to shoot my own film.

I started in acting. As a child I was a classically trained stage actor, but I always wanted to be in movies. When I was nineteen years old I went to

Los Angeles because of the film *River's Edge* (1987) that Crispin Glover was in. I was interested in his acting style. It was the most exciting thing I had ever seen—kind of like the way I felt when I first saw James Dean. I thought it was a great performance. I realized, "Wow—this is something new that I've never seen." It was a different kind of movie, a different kind of approach. I ended up reading this article about him and found out his dad was an acting coach, so I thought, "When I get to L.A. I'm going to look up his dad 'cause I gotta figure this out." So I went out there and trained with Bruce Glover for a year, and that was the greatest thing that ever happened. He was just incredible. His whole method and his whole way of approaching acting was a revelation to me. Then I did a bunch of work as an extra and couldn't really get anywhere. I was nineteen years old and didn't really know what I was doing.

I left Los Angeles because I was out of money and homesick and had no job. I split and came back to Atlanta and started to play music and did some more plays, always thinking, "One day I want to do film."

I learned when I was an extra on *thirtysomething* that I was still interested in acting, but I noticed right away that on TV the acting is way less than I was used to in theater. It's not that interesting to watch. And I started getting interested in the director. I noticed what the director was doing, and it didn't seem like he was doing anything. I thought, "OK, what's he doing?" And I got really infatuated with directing. But then I sort of forgot about it and pursued music for six or seven years. But the whole time, I was studying films. I got into French New Wave like Godard and Truffaut, and I got into all the neorealist American stuff that everybody gets into—Coppola and some of Dennis Hopper's stuff.

Then I got really into David Lynch and Alfred Hitchcock. And those were the two that stuck. Crispin was the one who told me, "You've got to see David Lynch." When I met him he was in this movie that Lynch directed called *Hotel Room*. Just amazing. He told me, "You've got to see *Eraserhead*." I had never seen *Eraserhead*, so I saw it, and that was the beginning of this infatuation that I still have with Lynch. He's my main person that I look to in film besides Hitchcock. So anyway, to make a short story long, I didn't go to film school.

I like to read, so I read a lot of books. I knew enough from acting about how to deal with actors, and I knew what they were going through. I didn't understand what a director did at all. So I started reading books and learned about the axis line, the 180 rule. I learned about composition and staging. I'd studied some independent films, and some of them excited me on one level but not completely. So I knew I had to make a film like Lynch's where there's a lot going on. That's why I ended up going with Jim Hunter. And when I found that Jim was really into Ridley Scott, I was really excited—because of *Blade Runner* and *Alien*. We decided to make a film that looks like *Blue Velvet* meets *Blade Runner*. I don't know if we did it or not.

The Initiate is absolutely my first film. I never did any shorts. I went straight from being a theater actor to being a film director. I made this huge jump. There's this huge chasm in between. Most people make short films—which I highly recommend. I wish I had done it. I'm glad I did what I did, but if somebody came up to me and said, "Hey, do you think I should make a short before I make a feature?" I would say, "Definitely."

As far as school goes, I personally don't know if I would have benefited greatly from film school mainly because I'm not a very scholarly person. I never did well in a school setting. I think that I would have probably learned a lot. I would have learned the same stuff I learned from reading, but probably faster and better. But I think that actually doing it was a better way for me to learn. That's how it's always been in everything else I've done. But I don't discourage film school. It just didn't ever line up for me, and I didn't want to have to wait. I just started doing it.

3

Financing—The Money Pit

Independent filmmaking is not for the faint of heart. As their moniker implies, independents opt for creative freedom, but this liberation wears a sometimes daunting price tag. However, with the currency native to the independent trade—passion, prayer, and the kindness of strangers—films do find their way from mental imagery to images on a screen.

Before any film sees the light of an HMI (Hydrargyrum Mercury Iodide), the business of money must be addressed, detailed, and attacked. Even if you never pay full price for bodies, services, or equipment for your film, you must eventually pay the bottom line. But while money may be scarce, it is also everywhere.

As these filmmakers attest, budget hunger is fed by knocking on doors, asking family and friends, winning grants, fund-raising, saving, pillaging your savings, mortgaging your house, selling stock in your film, and selling your film. Their budgets encompassed media from shorts to features, from Hi-8 video to 35mm, and from $50,000 to just under $1 million. And through travail and triumph, they all got made.

The crew shooting *Driven* on Ventura Boulevard (from left): Sound Mixer George Goen II (with camera), Director Michael Shoob, Script Supervisor Tim Dobson, Boom Operator Von Varga, Director of Photography Joseph Mealey, and 1st AC David Kiser.

Michael Shoob

I would say that the movie was in the seven-figure range—perhaps $800,000 to $1 million. When I began, I was hoping to make the film for about $400,000 but probably spent twice that. I continued to raise money during and after production. For example, we recut the movie after Toronto and before the Hamptons. We spent a fair amount on sound postproduction, hired a very good sound supervisor (and his team), and mixed at a good house. We shot a lot of footage with two cameras. We did multiple takes because of the importance of the performances.

Actually, the money came in from all different kinds of sources, but I think the important point is not whether Joe Blow Entertainment came up with an advance for foreign or that there were x-number of private investors who ponied up x-amount of money. The important point— which I can't emphasize enough—is that one must develop the mindset that, "This picture is going to get made." If one goes into private practice as a doctor or opens a pet shop, the financing is going to come from somewhere, and if more money is needed because the shop is teetering after the first or second year, you find the extra money or you fold.

You have to do whatever it takes. You raise money. You negotiate and keep negotiating with vendors and crew. If you need more money, you buy time until you can find the money. If you can't find the money you thought you would need, you rethink the scope of the film or the strategy for a particular scene. There are those who believe that these financial compromises kill a film. And then there are those who believe that having to make the financial compromises force a filmmaker to continue to assess and reassess what the film is about, and the film improves because of the additional scrutiny. Do you need fifty vehicles to make the scene work, or could five do just fine? Can you come back after two months of post and shoot the scene when there's money available?

The money was raised over a number of years by knocking on doors, picking up every lead, selling, begging, and cajoling. And much of the financing was raised after shooting began because the film's needs kept growing larger. And if you're the director, you don't want to shortchange yourself after so many years of waiting for the opportunity.

I think the biggest decision that has to be made is whether you're going to undertake to make the movie yourself. Bob Young made *Caught* when he found money in his DGA (Director's Guild of America) pension plan. He's seventy years old and he used his pension money. He didn't wait until all the pieces came together. He made the film any way he could.

Once your resolve is in place, there are numerous difficult, seemingly impossible obstacles to work through. But the toughest thing is to commit in the first place. For me, it became very clear that if I walked away from making this film I would regret it for the rest of my life.

Jennifer Farmer

I will be referring to the two films that I completed as producer/director. The first is called *The Incredible Pumpkin Man,* which is designed to be a half-hour TV series or special family film. The second is a feature film called *Naturally Native.*

On *Pumpkin Man* I was very fortunate to be able to go to friends and family. Because it was relatively low budget—it was right at the $100,000 mark—I was able to gather money from family and friends who had known me for a long time and who had done very well financially for themselves. I knew I needed to put together a director's reel—that is always a good place to start.

I didn't feel that the kind of clean, wholesome family story that I was going to tell would do well at film festivals. Many of the festivals are interested in dark, dysfunctional, heavy, violent, twisted, alternative kinds of things. And I thought, "Gee, what am I going to do with this thing?" Someone said to me, "Well, why don't you make a half-hour kid video out of it?" And of course, being involved with the Disney Company, I know there is a market for kid videos so I thought, "You know, that's a good idea." Then I was having dinner with another friend in the business who said, "If you're going to do that, why not go all the way and make a half-hour television special?" So that's kind of how it happened.

I was able to say to my investors, "Here's something I'm doing that's not just a director's reel, but something that I think we can all make money back on in the long run." I think as wonderful as art is, patrons of the arts like to get their money back. And I knew the people I was talking to would want that. So that was our original approach.

Fund-raising took a frighteningly short amount of time. Within about six weeks I had all the money I needed. I had put together a very detailed business plan: This is the script; these are the people I have attached to it (celebrity stars and crew, that kind of thing); this is why I think it will work. I had it all in three-ring binder form, and so as business people they were able to look at it and see what we were doing.

The budget was about $100,000. But by the time we were done with the film—because we needed to go back in and get a lot more money for post—we ended up with about a $165,000 budget. That includes the deferments that people worked for.

There's no reason to get half a movie done. Half a movie is no movie. We waited until we had pretty much everything in the bank so we could proceed.

Did I ask for deals? Absolutely. I would recommend it to anybody. First of all, if you have a really good solid script—good storytelling and something that has an interest and appeal for most people—there are people in Hollywood and in the world who want to be a part of that. They can see the success right there on the page.

As far as deals, my friends in the business were invaluable. We were able to get a free camera package from Panavision. Also, a very dear friend of mine owns a large post house here in Hollywood, and he donated $80,000 worth of free postproduction to me. He basically gave me a room with a Lightworks machine in it and said, "Help yourself. Have a good time. Let me know what you need." He did the Telecine transfers because we shot *Pumpkin Man* on super-16mm. We got a free jib-arm camera, free Lumicrane, and free Steadicam—a friend of mine was a Steadicam operator. I also got a free sound package from a dear friend of mine.

Everybody likes to think that they're backing a winner. When they see that you are very organized; that you have a good plan, a good idea, and a great passion for what you're doing; and that it looks like you're going to succeed—through your totally organized approach to things—people want to help and to give back in this business.

On *Pumpkin Man* we used the new Kodak stock. Kodak was very creative with us and very helpful to us. When they knew we were shooting super-16mm at night they gave us their best stock for that.

Denise Crosby called me on the phone and said, "I've heard about this picture and would really like to be a part of it. Can we meet for lunch?" Well, certainly having celebrities in your film really opens the eyes of the buyers, and that was a good idea. I met with her, and I knew that she was absolutely right to play the part of Mrs. Holloway, the mother in the film. I was delighted to have her on board. I'd had the pleasure of working with a lot of very good actors and crew people, and when it came time to do this I was able to call upon them.

For *Naturally Native*, I'll just back up a bit and say Valerie Red Horse was the executive producer on that. Hers is an Indian story of three Native American sisters set in present-day California. She hooked up with the Pequot tribal nation that runs the Foxwoods Casino in Connecticut, one of the largest most profitable casinos in the world today. They were looking to get into the entertainment world. They had a strong belief in Valerie's story and the things it was saying. She secured that financing in a matter of months. Again, we went to post houses and qualified crew and said, "Come on the journey with us. Come be part of something that we think is special and meaningful and magical and that is going to be both important and entertaining to people on down the line." That was the case both with *Pumpkin Man* and *Naturally Native*—we invited people to come be a part of it. Basically no one told us no. So asking is a good thing.

We didn't have to compromise on anything because I think having a strong vision as a filmmaker is not something you should have to compromise on. Perhaps I didn't get to shoot on the back lot of Paramount Studios, but we found ways to shoot and make it very believable and real and good. Again, having a lot of on-set experience and training and having my education from UCLA really brought me to this with experience and an experienced eye. I had never directed, but I still certainly knew what the recipe was.

The major hurdles of course were related to being low budget—not enough time and not enough money. But I think probably with the exception of Jim Cameron there never was a picture or a director who said, "You know what? I really didn't need all that time to shoot that movie, and I really didn't need all that money." So knowing that, you just have to decide, "This is what I've got, and this is where I'm headed, and this is what it takes to make this picture and this story."

Ali Selim

I hadn't liked the process of begging for my art while making *Yonnondio*, and I didn't want to start that again. I set up a commercial production company to do special projects—commercials that were too low budget to be done in the traditional way. I found about five clients who would each have one or two projects a year, and I promised to save all of the profits to put toward a film wherein the actors moved their lips. We told the clients what we were up to—that my wife would run the productions from our house, that there would be no cellular phone at their disposal and no smoked salmon on the set—and they all loved it.

Some of our clients hit the big time with large-budget jobs from Coca-Cola and IBM, and it wasn't long before we had saved over $50,000.

We spent about a week talking with key crew and equipment houses. We couldn't afford to pay full book rates (or the film would have budgeted out at around $225,000), but we wanted to pay a reasonable portion that would make everything seem businesslike. That way, if I found success with the film it wouldn't be on the blood, sweat, and tears of the local crew people. Also, I was too tired to beg. I preferred to negotiate.

We ended up with a deal paying all the crew members equally at $50 a day plus 2.5 percent of any revenues the film earned. The percentage was viewed not as back-end but as protection insurance, guaranteeing that if I became a millionaire (not that anyone could off of a film like this), the crew would not be forgotten.

Traci Carroll

The range I always tell is that our film costs more than a used car and less than a film degree from American Film Institute (AFI).

I don't think we had all of the money before shooting began. In fact, I'm sure we didn't have all of it. But I had known, since the time I graduated college, that I was probably going to want to shoot a film. And I had no idea how to go about it at all. IMAGE sort of opened the door to that. Right about the time I got involved with IMAGE was the time I started receiving a regular salary. So I started saving money—I saved as much money as possible and put it in CDs or savings accounts or whatever because I knew it would be really expensive to make a film.

When Brian Turner proposed that we do a film together, it made the whole thing seem a lot more feasible because it would be both of us paying for it. So it would only cost me half as much for the same film. And because I had known him for a long time I felt like he was really the person to follow through and back it up and all that.

We had enough money to get through the first six days of shooting and that was basically just equipment rentals—being able to pay for the equipment. So we sat down with Jim Hunter and figured out how much it was going to cost. He gave us a really accurate picture of how much we were going to be paying, and we sort of paid as we went. Some of it went on credit cards, although I personally pay off my credit card every month. I don't like to run that 20 percent interest balance on my credit. So we would shoot, and we would pay who we could, and we would let the others go sixty days until we could scrape up some more money to pay those folks.

We shot during October and November and the first few days of December. Then we took a long break until February. By then, we had saved up more money. Also, we had sat down with what we had shot and tried to figure out how much more we were going to have to shoot and how we could work it into six more days. But we always paid as we went, so we got the production done.

We bought a flatbed—I think we were paying $250 every six months to this guy. The total was $2,000 for the flatbed, but it was the cheapest way for us to edit, by far, because we got to keep it when we were done.

Because the look of the film is so beautiful and Jim is so talented, I felt like it was ultimately worth the expense to get him every cool toy that he wanted in order to produce it. Between the two of us we would scrape up enough money every time a bill came due to get paid. Now we're on the downhill of it because now all we're paying for is the festival entries and that's so cheap compared to all the production costs.

David Zeiger

I did not get financing very well. *The Band* was basically a financial disaster. We got less than $20,000 in grants. We did a lot of fund-raising in the Decatur community, but I ended up putting in a lot of personal money, which I hadn't had to do on *Displaced in the New South*. My father also gave us some money for it—he really supported it very much, and he was a huge help to us. Without my money and my father's money we couldn't have made the film. At this point I think we have spent about $140,000, and we probably will never recover all the money we put into it. *POV* (PBS's filmmaker showcase *Point of View*) was a pretty good sale. We'll probably do some international because of that sale, but it won't be a blockbuster on international television. We'll do pretty well on educational sales, but educational sales are not huge amounts of money.

For *Displaced in the New South* I got a lot of money from public grants—in fact, for a budget of $120,000 we raised $80,000 in grants, and the rest of it we got through TV sales and education sales. I've actually made a little bit of money on that film.

I do have a partner in production—James Jernigan of Jernigan Productions. It is extremely important to get people working with you who know what they're doing and who have the equipment. I had met James when his sister was on the board of Actor's Express. When Actor's Express did a promo piece, he shot it for them, and I was involved in that because I did the still photography for Express. It turned out that James has always wanted to make documentary films, and he had worked with Bob Drew who is kind of the godfather of American Cinema Verité. He has a real love of doing that, but his business is contracting crews for television. He approached me at the premier of *Displaced* and said he'd love to work with me on a project. The great thing about the relationship is that here I am willing and able to go, after producing and developing good personal projects, and James wants to be involved doing that, and he's got the equipment, and he's got the know-how. It made for a really good marriage. I couldn't have done *The Band* without James. Plus, he's got a lot of insight into television and documentaries and how it works.

I've heard and I'm sure one of the main reasons people go to film school is to meet the people they'll be working with. You meet people who are going to be cinematographers, and you meet people who are really good at XYZ. If you don't go to film school you have to do that through other ways. In the course of doing these two films I've built up relationships with people and postproduction houses who like my work and who trust me.

A principle that I've worked on is to pay people as soon as you can because a lot of people are willing to work for free and help out on a project—including high-end postproduction houses—if they believe in the project. But no one wants to be used, and unfortunately a lot of the young beginning filmmakers tend to use people—not maliciously, but because they can't figure out any other way to do it.

IMAGE (Independent Media Artists of Georgia etc.), a nonprofit media arts center in Atlanta, was a big help with getting my foot in the door. Something to watch for when you're trying to get started is an organization like that. One of the things that IMAGE does is have a relationship with post houses that agree to do work for half price and that kind of thing. The way that works—it's kind of interesting—they do it, but you'll constantly get bumped, but they'll do the work at midnight. A lot of them are hesitant because they've been burned—people haven't paid them at all. So I think the way you get your foot in the door is to watch out for something like that, but you really have to make a serious effort to live up to your end of the bargain.

For example, Crosstown Audio mixed both *Displaced* and *The Band*— Eric knew them from his previous work and said they were really good guys and they liked helping out people on projects that they were interested in. But you have to work at those kinds of relationships—you have to really pay attention to their needs. When people are doing favors for you, you have to always know they're doing favors for you, and you have to make them know how much you appreciate them. I think that's a big failing in that a lot of people take that for granted, and then they don't have it anymore.

Right now independent film is very hot. So people know that if the project is good and they do favors for it and help it get done, then later on down the road it's going to help them out, too. A lot of post houses are very interested in that. They have a self-interest in it, too. Crosstown is a good example. It was not at all self-serving, but Crosstown sent out a card before the *POV* broadcast of *The Band*. It had a picture of me leaning over the wall with a line leading down to Mary Ellen and Danny, and it said, "How did this father hear his son?" And then on the back it said, "He mixed his film at Crosstown Audio." And then it announced the air date. That was just wonderful. And we both benefited tremendously from the whole experience, even though I paid half price and they didn't make a ton of money—they made some, but they didn't make a ton. But it's that kind of thing—you have to work at developing that kind of relationship, and it's going to be easier in some places than in others. But I think those kinds of relationships are very possible to build anywhere—in any city.

Companies get into indie projects because their people want to be creative. They're creative people, but out of economic necessity they end up doing industrials for such-and-such screw manufacturer because that's where the money is. But a lot of people will jump at the chance to work on something that has some heart to it. So you have to go into it with the idea that you're offering people something. And if you've got a good project then you're offering people the chance to be involved in something that's good. People want to do that.

Chris Blasingame

Roadrunner—I wrote it; I directed it; I was there for the editing. I was there for every step basically.

I produced it with Mark Yoder, my friend, my longtime friend. I started an S-corporation, and I sold stock in the company to finance this thing. It's a good way to do it because tax-wise it's pretty easy for the investors. But as realities set in, the obvious thing was that the money was still going to come from friends and family. Very little of the stock that we sold was to people who actually thought they were going to make money. I sold most of it to friends and family, and I'm still raising it through friends and family. But I contacted a lot of people and they contributed in some way. And as much as I think it's a viable business proposition and that there's money to be made, to this day I think they think it's a contribution to the arts.

My initial budget was $60,000, and it will be up to $75,000 through the final print. When I started I had enough to get a week's worth in the can. I needed another day, but I didn't have another day, and I knew that going in because the schedule was very tight. The shoot was butted up against Labor Day and only a few people could stay. That's why I've had all the little reshoots here and there since. We intended to have a day to shoot the car and a lot of things. I jumped into it blindly and then I had to problem-solve by picking up things here and there.

I should have probably picked a smaller project to do. Features have been made for the amount I spent on this movie, but I didn't want to work that way—I wanted to put it up on the screen. I never agreed with Robert Rodriguez—I never thought that was sane thinking because, if you don't have the script and if you don't have the production value, then you have a big pile of crap. I always laugh at people who say, "I'm going to make a feature for $50,000." Usually it doesn't get done, and usually it looks like crap, and they won't make money off of it. So after realizing all that, I thought I would make a shorter movie for the same amount of money. I planned to have the camera car for a day, to have the grip truck, and to pay people so they wouldn't mutiny on me—although they did anyway because, once you pay people, they expect to be paid even more.

So I decided to make *Roadrunner* for the money, and I didn't have all the money that I knew I was going to need. Right now I'm pretty much on my estimate—I may have to go $15,000 over budget. But I didn't have all the money, and I jumped into it blindly because I knew it was going to get done one way or another. I wish I had had all the money in the bank before I got started—it would have been finished by now.

Chad Etchison

We actually financed *The Initiate* ourselves, which was very excruciating. I don't know which would be worse—I didn't even try the finding money route. I know that's hell, and my attitude was, "If I'm gonna make this film and it sinks, I don't want to put anybody else on the ship with me except for my wife. Put her on the ship but nobody else, by God." So we ended up mortgaging a house. We were in a lucky position—we had access to some money that most people don't have. That made a big difference. Even though it was low budget, we had the ability to get hold of money on a level which most beginning filmmakers couldn't. So that was another key.

Several things had to fall together to make it work. Originally, I thought the budget was going to be $30,000. It ended up going into the quarter-million dollar range. It could climb as high as $300,000 after post. I still have to do an answer print. I still have to do sound. *Post*—which I'm doing now—is costing me nothing because I own a Steenbeck and I'm cutting it myself, along with Mary and Jim Hunter, who is volunteering his time.

I wanted to shoot it on 35mm, but we shot it on super-16mm, so that was the first big compromise. It saved a lot on film costs alone—one 400-foot roll of 16mm is about $117, which is about eleven to twelve minutes of screen/film time. And a five-minute mag of 35mm is over $400. Processing is about the same for 16mm and 35mm. The only thing that you can save on with 35mm is that they usually print specific takes, whereas for 16mm they just print the whole deal. I'd say 35mm film stock is about triple the cost of 16mm, and camera rental is twice the cost. It would have tripled the budget to shoot 35mm. It was never even a consideration.

I bought a regular 16mm Arri SR and had it converted to super-16mm. I paid the same amount of money that it would have cost to rent it, so I figured I'd buy it. I thought about buying an Arri BL-1 because they're about the same cost, but it has all kinds of problems—it's a bulky camera—it's a loud camera. I didn't want to start the film and not be able to finish it. Everybody was also telling me, "Oh you're a first-time filmmaker. You've got to shoot 16mm or you'll be skipping a step." So I let some of that pressure affect me, too. I was very aware of this lack of experience first-time filmmaking thing, too. You're acutely aware of that on your first film. Everybody reminds you.

I bought the camera, and we rented a series of prime lenses—we used a mix of 35mm and 16mm super speed prime lenses. Those were really expensive. We didn't want to use the zoom lens because the zoom lens breathes and you don't get the clarity at each focal length. Since we were hoping it would get blown up we wanted it really tight. We also used really low-speed film stock—100 ASA 7248—which was crucial to the look of the film. It provided really rich blacks and tight colors.

I also bought a Dedo kit, which is a small lighting kit, and I bought the Steenbeck. I bought a Nagra machine that broke the first week, so we had to rent a stereo Nagra. The rest of the stuff we rented. We rented a five-ton grip truck, and we rented supplemental lighting and dollies—we did a lot of rental stuff. I did own the camera and the Dedo kit and the Nagra, but other than that we had to rent.

The rental house, even though they're a big commercial outfit, really came to the table—they gave us two and a half days. They slashed their prices more than half and really helped us out. We got lower deals because I think their philosophy is It's better to have the stuff out there than sitting around making nothing. At least on these independent things. The lab also cut us a really good deal. So I think if independent filmmakers knew that these people will come to the table and help them, it would seem less daunting and intimidating. Because financing a film is a daunting thing.

4

Preproduction—
Cents and Sensibility

Every ship has a course. Every battle has a strategy. Every film has pre-production.

Preproduction is priceless. It costs you nothing, yet it can save you incalculable dollars, Tylenols, and even your film. Essentially, you craft your film for the first of many times in preproduction. You orchestrate all the players, locations, equipment, cast, crew, and props to anticipate and forestall any complications once film is rolling.

Preproduction tends to be benign, even fun. You fantasize, you theorize, you mentally make your movie countless times, picturing how all your resources will come into play. But as blissfully safe as this time may seem, by its very nature, dress rehearsal must end, and the curtain must rise.

Michael Shoob

The short version is that writing the script was very hard; raising the money was not easy; and after that, any preproduction or production issue, no matter how difficult, wasn't as hard as the first two. Because you're *making the film*. What drives you crazy during the writing and fund-raising is the nagging feeling that you won't get there. Ever. The more folks we had hired, the better I felt.

The movie, as has been my experience with a number of scripts, went through all kinds of incarnations. When I first began writing it, it seemed that it was going to be a straight-ahead chronicle of my experiences as an L.A. cabdriver. Then, over the years, I tried making it a romantic comedy involving a writer-cabdriver. Then, I was sure it should be a political thriller involving cabdrivers. Finally, when I was certain that I was going to make it independently, I tried to go back to my original notion and make something that interested me. The only drawback about writing something personal—as other filmmakers have also told me—is that you never know how you're doing. There is no benchmark, really. So I was writing without any certainty that *Driven* would interest an audience. When I finished, however, and passed the script around, it quickly became apparent that the script had worked—at least for a number of people.

Now, some thoughts on who I hired: My cameraman, Joe Mealey, had been an AFI (American Film Institute) fellow with me, and he had shot my 35mm short, *The Companion*. *Driven* was his first feature, but I knew he could do a terrific job with it and that our understanding of one another would be very helpful. The producer, Daniel Linck, had just produced a pilot for PBS. I liked his sensitivity and generosity of spirit. I thought he had a terrific willingness to give everything he had to *Driven*. Both of these guys were still helping the show two years after. The production designer, Patti Podesta, had strong feature credits as the number-two art department person, and she was ready to make the move to running the department. She also was on the faculty at Art Center and at USC, so she was great at articulating what she wanted to do. She had also, by pure coincidence, edited one of my projects at AFI (I had lost touch with her in the meantime), so we had worked together before. The editor, Fabienne Rawley, seemed to be on a lot of lists as a future star in her field, and she had a reputation for liking independent films. She had edited a feature for director George Sluizer (*The Vanishing*) and has done another one since. I chose her over

(From left) Best Boy Electric/2nd Unit Gaffer J. D. Bishop, Director Michael Shoob, (with megaphone), Gaffer James Sweeney, and 1st AD Brent Bowman confer during the shoot.

a more experienced editor. I just thought she had the right sensibility for the picture.

In short, one of the great dimensions of making the film was bringing a group of talented, thoughtful folks together. And I have continued to solicit their opinions almost daily for the last two years. It's also a tribute to them that they were very respectful and supportive of one another.

About casting: We took a great deal of time in casting the picture because, much to the chagrin of my mostly patient casting directors, I insisted on seeing large numbers of actors for each role, and I had numerous callbacks. For what should probably be called the female romantic lead, I read fifty-five women, mostly because I was searching for a specific quality that seemed to be very hard to find. For the wife of one of my leads, I did numerous callbacks with very fine actors—I just wanted to make sure. My feeling then and now is that casting is a huge piece of what you do as a director. I took my time, a great deal of time.

Let me take you through the process. We first hired a casting director. We interviewed a number of potential candidates and ended up with
Mark Tillman, who had worked mostly on movies of the week. I think
Mark was intrigued by the script and also liked the idea of working on
an independent film.

Let me also say that directors are probably a little haunted by their
most recent experience, and I was determined not to repeat what had
happened on my short film. I had cast a very fine actor named Delroy
Lindo (who has gone on to do *Crooklyn* and many other things), but we
had never met. He flew from New York to Las Vegas to shoot my short.
And I'll just say that we could never find any common ground or understanding about what the project should be. With hindsight, I think he
was probably right about many things. But, most significantly, what I
learned was that I had to meet any actor who would be in a film of mine.
I would want to make sure that we basically could work together, that
we understood the parameters of budget and the rest of it. And I probably wanted to just test my feelings about the actor as a human being. Or,
just plainly, is this someone I feel good about? Paul Mazursky talks
about wanting to hang out for days or a weekend with the folks he is
considering casting, and I think he's got the right idea.

Now, I also want to say that I think casting represents a huge percentage of what you bring to the table as a director. Unfortunately, many
directors inherit a package and end up forfeiting much of this role, but
let's just say that in an indie film you've got more flexibility.

So, broadly speaking, I was looking for a thirty-five to fortyish black
man, a thirtyish Jewish bookie, a slightly reserved observer guy, and a
young, fresh-faced exuberant cabdriver.

Now, in some ways, LeGrand, the young guy, was the easiest. I saw
something out of Melville—like Bartleby or Terence Stamp in the Peter
Ustinov film, *Billy Budd* (1962). And the fact is, the one actor I imagined
when I was writing the guy is Chad Lowe, who impressed the hell out of
me in the *Life Goes On* series. He was Legrand. I mentioned this to Mark

Tillman, who happened to have a way to get him the script. Chad read it and came to meet, and we liked each other, and hey, it was easy!

Unfortunately, I didn't have any other person so clearly visualized, and I had over thirty other characters to cast.

For Pelton, I had liked Tony Todd—ironically enough, where I really liked him was in a remake of *Night of the Living Dead*. He brought a real humanity to that B-movie. He read the script in New York and liked it enough to call me immediately and say he was interested. But two things made me hesitate. One, I would have to commit to him without meeting first. The second was that I wanted to explore alternatives. After reading countless actors and flirting with someone we were very interested in—"He's coming to meet you today. No, he's not coming," and so on day after day—I decided to cast Vondie Curtis Hall who had been terrific in *Passion Fish* (1992) and who my friend at *Chicago Hope* assured me was as great as he seemed to be when we met.

Again, I was determined, based on an earlier experience, not to cast a single actor who wouldn't or couldn't meet with me. This sounds obvious, but with numbers of actors and their agents, there is a great deal of "We won't meet without an offer." And you reply that you will "make an offer pending a meeting."

Meanwhile, I was back and forth, reading dozens of men for the bookie including one well-known comedian who was so disinterested in the audition that I had to ask him if he resented reading for me. Finally, Vondie Curtis Hall's manager offered up Judd Nelson, who met with me and told me he loved the script. I liked the idea of Judd because the character is something he's never done before. I thought he might surprise a lot of people, and I felt that could be very interesting. I had a good feeling, but I was wrong.

After reading many, many people, we finally began putting together our ensemble, but were still having a very hard time finding our "observer." It looked like it was going to be Whip Hubley, who is a little more handsome than I was imagining for the character. But despite our endless auditions of other actors and endless conversations with agents, Whip just seemed destined to be in the movie. He wasn't quite what I had imagined, but he just kept popping up in my psyche.

Now, if you had told me what was going to happen next, I wouldn't have believed in a million years it could happen on an independent film. The manager of two of the actors said he didn't like the idea of casting Hubley. I told him that everybody had been cast. I had told Whip that he was in the picture, and I wasn't going back on my commitment. But the manager repeated that he was serious. And guess what? He pulled his actors.

We had cast everybody and now we were going to have to push back our start date to begin casting again for two roles.

So Tony Todd finally came to town and wanted to do it, and I said "yes" after finally meeting him. He looked just like Pelton to me.

Then for the bookie, Dan Roebuck just knocked everybody's socks off in the audition. Dan had portrayed the killer in *River's Edge* and would later play Jay Leno in *Late Shift* for HBO, right after *Driven*. He plainly won the part. He wanted it badly. My producer, Dan Linck, believes to this day that this was providence—that Todd and Roebuck (who've gotten stunning reviews) were meant to play these roles—and maybe he's right.

I believe strongly that one should be a near perfectionist in casting even the smallest roles. Because day players make the movie—they give it an authenticity, a reality. I'm very proud of Milo Addicas (who was a terrific angry passenger) and Blake Sopers (a knife-wielding kid) who really gave *Driven* a great deal of its character, its grit.

Jennifer Farmer

I cannot emphasize enough how important preproduction is. Planning your flight and flying your plan are really what preproduction is all about. In a lot of ways your movies will take place in preproduction. You need to have your script absolutely locked so that every word is important, makes sense, and is part of telling the story.

Preproduction, of course, involves casting. After you have the world's greatest script, you need the world's greatest cast. If an actor can really bring something to your film in talent and in believing in the project and in believing in what you're doing and trying to accomplish, then there's a way to work around the agent weasels and put the deal together to make it work. And you can always make deals with points and deferments and back-end profits. Whenever possible, I feel it's important to go directly to the actor. Once they fall in love with the project they will tell their managers and lawyers and agents that, "I will be doing this. So cooperate with these people." So that's a very good thing to do. You want like-minded cast members who see the vision of what you're doing.

So then it's planning your locations. Planning the schedule. Planning all the shots. I don't storyboard. That's not really part of my process.

Winging it and guerrilla filmmaking are the two most frightening phrases in filmmaking. They should not exist. They should never take place. It's not a good thing. I feel very strongly that everything needs to be very organized and in place. All the paperwork needs to take place and everyone needs to be on the same page. We had lots of preproduction meetings in both films to coordinate what was happening and who was doing what. My process is very collaborative. I like to work with the director of photography and with the sound person, having them go on the scouts to the locations and ask if we are under some dire troubles here. Of course, the first AD (assistant director) and all the department heads and everybody gives their input about what is good and bad in the situation, and we make amendments accordingly.

I wanted this to be not just an opportunity for me to first-time direct on *Pumpkin Man* or to first-time feature direct on *Naturally Native*. I wanted it to be a good opportunity for everyone involved. It's very important to do that. I couldn't talk to people about making a film without talking about what was good for them. In low-budget filmmaking, everyone who's there is doing you a favor or doing the project a favor, but we can't have anyone present who has the attitude of "I'm doing you a favor," because you can never get right with those people. It's never

45

Naturally Native celebrates the wrap of the shoot. (Left to right) Jennifer Farmer, Mary Kay Place, and Valerie Red Horse (codirector).

enough for them. Something's always wrong. And ill will spreads like wildfire through a film crew on a set.

My process is to be very family oriented. We are a family when we are making a film, and everyone is to be honored and to be spoken to kindly. There's lots of please and thank you, and there's lots of hugging and that kind of thing. It needs to be a very happy place.

I would go to people who had been in the art department or the set decorating department before and who needed an opportunity and a credit to become key in their department. One of my electricians needed an opportunity to be Best Boy. You say to these people, "Here's an opportunity. I'm not going to pay you a whole lot of money, but here's the opportunity that I can provide for you. I'll give you an opportunity so that you can use this as experience or whatever on your résumé so that you can go forward and advance your career just as I'm wanting to do mine." And everyone really came on board with that. There were people who didn't need the credit and didn't need the help, but they really believed in the project. They either loved Halloween, or they loved their children, or they loved that this was a good project.

It is important to present the opportunity to these people in the same way that you present it to your investors—that this is an opportunity to be part of something special, magical, and wonderful that will matter. And be very sincere—it is really important when you're putting your group together. This paradigm was especially true in the case of *Naturally Native*. It was very groundbreaking in that it was a feature film about Native Americans in present-day—instead of that god-awful stereotypical kind of thing that's always been presented in John Wayne movies.

The director/DP/editor relationships all have to be very solid and very good. We have to be finishing each other's sentences and be on the same page with what we're doing and with the vision. If I have an idea but someone has a better idea let's go with that—or if my vision of the film doesn't incorporate that, then we'll go with that. It needs to be a very friendly exchange. And both on *Pumpkin Man* where my DP was Kelly McGowan, a friend of mine from college, and on *Naturally Native*—where my DP was an Emmy award-winning very talented man by the name of Bruce Finn who wanted to get into feature film shooting—we all worked very well together and had a delightful relationship.

I don't believe in dictatorship. I believe everybody comes to the party with a lot to say that's important. I'm sort of the final say or sounding board of the way things will be, but I really like it when people offer good input.

Rehearsing with the cast is the equivalent of good preproduction. It's also important to hire a good, competent, well-focused cast—they don't even have to be really experienced. The four kids that I had as leads on *Pumpkin Man* didn't have resumes that were a mile long. But I cast these people because they were these characters in real life, and I was going to be able to work with them in that way. For example, Christopher Ogden did not have a current relationship with his father; I don't believe he had met his father. In *Pumpkin Man,* Christopher's character is dealing with the loss of his father—his parents have gotten divorced and he has to face his favorite holiday without his favorite person, his father. From a humanities standpoint I was wanting to evoke emotions in Christopher

Left to right: Jennifer Wynne Farmer, Tiffany Ellen Solano (as "Jenn"), and Jennie O-Hara—the three Jenn's, with Christopher Ogden on the set of *Pumpkin Man.* © Pumpkin Pictures LLC.

and yet not harm him emotionally and bring up issues that maybe he hadn't properly dealt with or never dealt with regarding his own father. I wanted this to be a good experience for him, and it was. There was a way to do that.

With the three sisters in *Naturally Native*—we were now dealing with them as adults, but the movie started with them as children—I said, "You know, I'd like to do a sit-down with the three of you. I'll be Barbara Walters and interview you three and ask questions about the movie. And we'll sort of discover these characters and learn their history together." It really worked out wonderfully because we found there were some areas of discretion that we worked on together as a family and found a way to answer all these questions. They found they had questions as well, so we were focusing on being on the same page.

It is every actor's responsibility to show up to the set knowing her lines and knowing who they are. I'm certainly happy to answer questions about character and motivation, but it's very important to spend time in rehearsal talking about character, motivation, what the scene means, why it exists, what we're doing in the scene, why it's important, and how that moves the story along. We spent a lot of time doing that. I don't want to do it to death because I don't want to ruin the spontaneity of what's going to happen when the camera's rolling. But you can see it in the actor's eyes when there's a full awareness of what they're bringing to the character or when there still needs to be some clarity.

I enjoy spontaneous performances. There's a part in *Naturally Native* where the character Tonya is talking about being privy to the fact that, due to alcoholism, her mother died giving birth to her. She's always blamed herself. When we got to shooting the film she broke down and was crying, and it was a wonderful performance. I wasn't expecting that, but boy it really worked in the scene and it was a nice treat. If you use good actors, give them some leeway, and convey to them the confidence you have in them, they will give you little gems and little moments. A good actor will give you a slightly different spin and a slightly different performance on every take to give you choices in editing, which is a real treasure.

As I was shot-listing each scene, I would do the broad strokes of blocking. We know that we need to start over here and end up there, so we need to cross over at this point. I was told by a director one time to trust the actor's feet. When the actor feels he needs to move away or move to or move whatever, usually that's a good motivation. Go with that. I had broad-stroked blocking provided for them on my shot list, and I would say, "Stay here, and move here." Or "I think he would do this in motivation because . . . but if you disagree just let me know." I don't want to create robots. I want them to be free to give their talented performance, but we needed to have some idea of what was going on because in low-budget filmmaking, you need to show up, know what you're doing, shoot, and leave. There's really no time to hem and haw and discuss all that kind of stuff. That needs to take place in rehearsal or during the preproduction process.

Rehearsal depends on how much access you have to your shooting space. We shot *Pumpkin Man* in my house and *Naturally Native* in Valerie's house so we had access to the places we were going to be shooting, and that was very *very* beneficial.

I think in the way that Olympic athletes are always nervous right before they are going to perform in the Olympics, and yet they have spent their lives preparing for it—that's how I was feeling as I began both *Pumpkin Man* and *Naturally Native*. I was ready. I had prepped it out. I had thought it out. I had lived it, dreamed it, and breathed it twenty-four hours a day for the months of preproduction. I was ready to go—there was nothing left to do (otherwise don't shoot). Shooting day had arrived and I just needed to go do it. I realized I needed to be flexible to the changes that would occur while shooting, but I had that plan in mind. I felt very prepared. On both shows as we got ready to shoot I was ready to go, and I was happy to go and excited to go and inspired to go. What I found interesting was that, as a first-time director, on neither occasion did I feel any anxiety or insecurity or a "What am I doing here?" kind of thing. It felt like the most natural thing in the world. Even more than learning to walk—it felt like I belonged there. I was happy to be there. I was excited to be there, and I was ready to see it happen.

Ali Selim

I hit the books and the literary magazines. I finally remembered *Emperor of the Air*, the Ethan Canin story from nearly ten years prior. I re-read it and contacted his agent. We began a seven-month negotiating process that took more in legal fees than in the final option payment and yielded a slim two-page document. This was actually the longest part of making the film. Everything after that was simple.

I made some notes on the story. My producing and writing partner, Tom Lieberman, and I rewrote the story into movie structure but not script form. I spent about a month with these forty pages just reading and thinking, and then wrote the script in one day. I rewrote three or four of the scenes later, during rehearsal with the two main actors.

We let the crew and cast pick Memorial Day 1995 and the six days that followed, plus the two days preceding the Fourth of July for production. They felt that there would be little work to turn down during this period, and the feeling turned out to be correct.

We put together a full crew with four electrics, four grips plus dolly, two ACs, craft services, catering, etc. If people were comfortable and fed and not overworked everything seemed less horrible. For me, I was making my film. But for the crew, it was the same old taking the dolly off the truck and putting the dolly back on. I think there was an energy on the set that made them feel differently, but that didn't change their job descriptions much.

The DP, Mike Welckle, and his gaffer, Ralph Lindell, who is also my brother-in-law, spent several days combing through the script making a shot list and ultimately a storyboard. Once we found the location—which was not easy, though it ended up being three blocks from my house (we found it only after scouting small towns up to one hundred miles away)—we hired an architect to draw scale plans of the two homes and the neighborhood. We then made a lighting plan for each of the storyboarded shots. It was a way to get the best equipment without having to guess. It ended up saving us an entire day during production because everyone had these plans and could work ahead two or three shots if we had enough lights and cable to spare. Efficient was a word used often. I don't recall making up anything on the set. It was all according to plan. I don't know that I would feel the need to be that tight if I were paying full board. I do feel, watching the film now, that there were some missed opportunities.

We signed a low-budget agreement with SAG (Screen Actors Guild), which was relatively easy to do, and Lynn Blumenthal Casting agreed to do a full casting. The film was designed around the performances of the two main characters with everyone else literally doing a two-hour cameo. We had scores of actors come to the auditions and no one questioned the situation. We ended up with two or three strong picks for every role and had to do callbacks twice, which everyone came to without complaint. Paul Boesing and Hon Schumacher made us laugh, so we booked them.

Paul Boesing, from *Emperor of the Air.* Photo by Mike Welckle.

Traci Carroll

I guess right after Brian and I started writing the script we went to see this film called *Barcelona,* a Whit Stillman film. And there's this excruciatingly long shaving scene in that film—it's like real-time shaving. And Brian said, "Oh that's so cool. I want to do a shaving scene in a movie." So we started working on this script sort of based around the idea that he wanted to do a shaving scene.

So then we thought, "Well are we going to shave with the little plastic razor that you see on the Gillette commercials? Or are we going to use shaving cream?" And we got this idea that we were going to use a lather cup, and the actor was going to put the lather on with a brush and use one of those double-edged razors that you have to stick the razor blade in and screw it down. We decided that would be so much more cool, and it would give the scene an anachronistic or timeless feel. Then we thought, "Why is this guy shaving?"

It was such an evolutionary process. I basically sat down one day and

Brian Turner as Guy in *Five O'clock Shadow*.

said, "OK, somebody's got to start. So I'll just start." I started writing and I mailed him ten pages. I think he hated pretty much everything that I wrote. So he edited out what he didn't like—just totally got rid of it and wrote in the stuff that he thought would be neat. Then he mailed it back to me. And I thought, "Oh I hate this." And we mailed it back and forth. I have all the drafts on my computer and we probably have over one hundred different draft versions of the script.

We knew there were certain things we wanted. We wanted the shaving scene. We wanted it to have this sort of timeless feel like when you can't really place if it was in the 1990s or in the 1950s. Film that has always been intriguing to me, because it's a visual medium, is silent film. So I really wanted to do a film that didn't have any dialogue in it. But we rethought that because films that don't have any dialogue are distracting because people don't understand them. People are too used to having dialogue. So we thought, "How can we tell the story and not have too much dialogue at all—like one line per character?" Then we decided that color was really important to our film, too. Since we weren't going to have a lot of dialogue, we wanted the color to represent the characters. So Veronica would be the red character and Guy would be the blue character. Whenever they were in an environment where they were in control or it was sort of their area, the color would reflect that. All the extras were black-and-white.

We decided that shaving would be part of this guy's dream—we would make it a dream sequence. We decided that the whole shaving thing would be a frustration dream for him; he'd be shaving, but none of the stubble would be coming off of his face; no matter how hard he would work at it, it wouldn't come off. And we envisioned this flash of Veronica in his dream, so we realized that she would be connected to his frustration. And it grew from that one bit. Who is she and how did he meet her? We give the audience clues of how they might have known each other, and you sort of see how they interact with each other, but we left our film intentionally abstract.

If you go to a museum and see a painting, you interpret that painting in a way that nobody else does—so it's your very own personal interpretation of this painting and what it means to you. In filmmaking, in strictly narrative type films you have a screenplay that tells you what's going on and you're just watching a story. I really wanted our film to be more interactive where people would look at it and say, "Well I think it means this, or I think it means that." So that's how we ended up with the story we had—we allowed our characters to make their own decisions and we didn't explain a lot to the audience.

I would say we worked on the script for nine months. That is probably a long time for a short film, but it was necessary because we didn't have dialogue to explain it, we were sitting down trying to hash out what the visuals were going to be, and we had to decide what we were going to include in the way of art department or props to help tell the story. And then there was also a lot of letting people read it and asking them what they thought about it. It had an ending that was really dumb, and I felt like it was very cliché. Then one day I had this idea for the ending

Lauri Faggioni as Veronica in *Five O'clock Shadow.*

of the film, but it was so bizarre I thought, "Well I'll just throw it out there to Brian and if he hates it then we'll just keep working on an end that's not as cliché as the ending that we've got right now." So I called him up and said, "OK what about this?" And he loved it—he thought it was really funny and really strange and it sort of went with what we were trying to do in that it left yet another thing for the audience to wonder about.

About three months after we started working on the script I met Jim Hunter at an IMAGE Christmas party and he asked, "Oh you're doing a film? What are you going to shoot it on?" And at that time we were just going to use my little 8mm camera because we didn't know what we were doing and knew nothing about lighting—we thought we'd check books out of the library and figure it out. Jim, who was the cinematography teacher and was on the board at IMAGE, basically volunteered to shoot our film. So I called Brian and told him, "Hey this guy at IMAGE is going to shoot our film for free and all we have to do is pay for the lighting equipment." Later we found out that the lighting equipment was way expensive, but at the time we thought it was a great deal, and it was.

So then Jim sort of became involved, and it was like having my own film tutor to tell me how to do my preproduction and who to call to be on the crew and what all the grip equipment was. He taught everybody on the crew what the grip equipment was. A lot of the people from our crew were people from his cinematography class who really wanted to work on a film and they knew nothing, but they were willing to give up their weekends to do it.

So we started working on the script in October. Probably the following July was when we were storyboarding and casting and putting together some of our preproduction stuff and trying to figure out locations and coordinating when everybody would be available to shoot. Brian was on overnights at CNN and we were trying to figure out how this would work with his schedule and all that.

Every single thing was storyboarded because Jim flat out told me, "I'm not going to shoot it unless I can see a storyboard of all the camera angles." I hated that; I did not want to do it. I thought, "Why can't you take the camera in and set it up and figure it out?" And then I realized the first day on set just what a valuable tool the storyboards were—how it was so great when I was standing there trying to set up the shot. I'd say, "OK, Lauri's going to be here and Brian's going to be here." And Jim would say, "Well do you want this kind of angle or this kind of angle?" And I would open up the storyboard and I'd say, "It's gonna look like this." And then he would know what lens to put on and where to position the camera so he would match all my storyboards. They aren't super great illustrations but the main thing in my storyboards was to show where the characters were, but also kind of what the lighting was going to be like—where the reds and the blues were—because those were the important colors.

Storyboards save you so much time on the set because you already know ahead what it's going to look like, and even more important, how it's going to cut together. I didn't really understand the whole editing

Script Supervisor, Wendy Mericle, and Director, Traci Carroll, go over storyboards of an upcoming scene.

process when we shot the film, but when we got into the editing room I started to realize how valuable it was that we had stuff that cut back and forth and didn't look funny. So I did all the storyboards. I did some in color and some in black and white. Jim helped me work through some of the technical problems, like, "If you want to shoot it this way then you need to think about X, Y, and Z before you get your heart set on that angle," or whatever.

We had two locations. We had approached the owner of a bar, and he was really into the idea of shooting a film at his place. That bar is not in existence anymore, but at the time he thought he would get a copy of our film and show it in a loop to some techno music and he was all excited about that. He was very accommodating. And the other location we shot in was Brian's apartment. We repainted his room a key wall blue color. And we repainted his sunroom, which was Veronica's room, with a really deep red. We even stained his floors so they would all match. Those were the two locations. It was difficult for Brian and his roommate because they were living in the set while we were shooting there, which was from the 17th of February to the 9th of March off and on, on weekends. And we had to go back a year later and reshoot all the love scene stuff when we realized our show was just not going to come together unless we reshot. We just knew we couldn't give up any of our props or the apartment until we were done, and I was hoping Jennifer Blix wouldn't break up with Brian—then we wouldn't have a body double. But that worked out too.

We did not audition, but if I had it to do over again, I would. Brian, of course, was great and we obviously didn't audition Brian because it was his project. His whole reason for doing the project was because he wanted to have a piece that showed off his acting abilities, and he wanted to be the lead character. In independent film, if you're an unknown, the only way to do it is to have your own film. So we knew Brian was going to be the lead and we just needed to find the right girl to play Veronica.

Lauri Faggioni was a friend of a friend of a friend, and she had been in one film—a student film—and she had the right look. I think, in retrospect, she wasn't the right type because the character had to be really bitchy, and she couldn't separate herself from the character. I would say, "You have to be more angry and more harsh—you can't smile and be nice." And she would say, "Well I just feel bad about being mean to Brian." And I'd tell her, "It's not you being mean to Brian—it's your character, and your character is kind of bitchy and that's not you and you need to separate that." But that was really hard for her. Now if I was going to do an audition I think it would be easy to tell if an actor was capable of reaching that range because I could give her a script to read from—so I could see how well she did. The other thing was, halfway through the film, she decided she wanted to be a writer instead of an actress so she lost a lot of the enthusiasm. I thought I was going to have to tie her down to keep her on the set the last day that we shot. We shot until four in the morning because I knew she was not coming back. There's actually this funny thing where Brian is supposed to be choking

Lauri, but the angle is behind the bed frame so you can only see the top of her head. She actually had gone home and we just laid the wig on the bed. There's this very funny behind-the-scenes footage of Brian choking the wig.

We rehearsed with a video camera and blocked out all the scenes with Lauri and Brian. Oddly enough all the stuff we rehearsed ended up not being shot at all. The original script was thirty-three pages, and the first day on the set when I realized how slow it was actually going to move in reality, I went home and cut it down to seventeen pages. So a lot of the stuff we had rehearsed ended up getting cut—the first part of the film ended up totally chopped off. Lauri and Brian took it upon themselves to sit and rehearse while we were setting up the shot. But having very few lines, there wasn't a lot of memorization—it was more blocking like, "I'm going to put the lighter down and you're going to pick the lighter up. And I'm going to lean forward and you're going to lean backward." It was choreographing what their actions were going to be instead of learning the lines.

Once we got to working just with Brian we didn't do any rehearsal because Brian had written the script and had the whole film in his head and knew exactly what was going on, and he didn't need rehearsal. That was a real advantage of working with the person who wrote the script. We sat down and talked about all the camera angles together, and between the two of us, we worked out every scene. He didn't need any rehearsal—it was just the other people who hadn't been there from the beginning of the process.

We shot on 16mm because, at the time we started making our film, 35mm was absolutely not a possibility because of the expense and because we didn't have access to the equipment in the same way that we had access to 16mm. And super-16mm is not a good festival format because if you want to have it projected at a festival—most festivals will only take stuff that's on 16mm or 35mm—you have to have your image blown up to 35mm or shrunk down to 16mm. And knowing that we would want to be able to project it and couldn't afford 35mm we decided to go ahead and shoot on 16mm. And since televisions are square it's the perfect aspect ratio. If our film was ever released on video there would be no cropping. It's the perfect size.

In the event that any of us become huge filmmakers and somebody wants a copy of our twenty-minute film for high definition television (HDTV), we will go back and crop it for that. But that's the only reason a lot of independent filmmakers are shooting films now, especially feature films, on super-16mm. If their films sell and they get a theatrical release, super-16mm is the same aspect ratio as 35mm and also as HDTV. So particularly for a feature film, super-16mm is the way to go. But for a short, where it's only going to find a life in festivals, it was the way to go for us. That's the main life of a short; they hardly ever get distributed on video. Only now with the Independent Film Channel are they starting to get broadcasted. If I were to do a feature tomorrow I would use super-16mm.

Chris Blasingame

I was preproducing *Roadrunner* from March up until we shot in September, but that was just me. I was prepared, but I was also ready to go onto the set and not know what to expect. I was pretty prepared and knew my material well enough—I had a lot of preproduction for myself. But then I dragged other people in. We had auditions in May. I think we started up in July and August with once-a-week meetings.

I did a storyboard, but nobody bothered to even look at it. It was all in my head, so I did this storyboard and distributed it to everybody who would make a difference. When I was working on films I always thought it would be nice to have one because you could know what your day would look like and foresee any problems on your job. So I did this thing and nobody looked at it. They commented on how nice it looked, but nobody really looked at it.

I went down to view the locations. Not all the locations were locked, but generally, they were. The general area was locked and we knew where the big scenes were. I planned the shots, but I don't believe in being so

Chris Blasingame directs George Wilson (left) as Roadrunner. Photo by Tim Sabo.

crazy that you can ever foresee all the details. Once you bring your actors and everybody in, it sort of takes on a life of its own. And if you stifle that life because you have some sort of preconceived notion, then you're killing that life. So it was fun to bring everybody in—we'd rehearse it and get it to a certain point. But once they're in the car and it's running down the road . . . you can't plan everything to death. So I had all the shots but they changed. They didn't change a lot. I knew the skeleton—I just needed to put the flesh on it. The final product didn't quite look like the storyboard but we got all the shots to satisfy the storyboard.

We rehearsed the big scenes. We didn't rehearse smaller scenes like the sheriff and the deputy—we let that go until the day of shooting. But we did rehearse the car scenes, which were long and needed a certain playing off of one another. Roadrunner, who is George Wilson, is amazing—when he walked into auditions he just blew us away with the monologue he brought in. He had a lot of different ideas as to what *Roadrunner* would be. As much as I didn't try to tell him "Roadrunner is this" because I didn't really know what it was either—he became it. As much as I didn't try to do that, we had to work on it a lot. So we needed rehearsal for that because those were big Roadrunner scenes. At one point he did it screaming every word, but that gets a little overbearing and you ask, "Why is he screaming every word?" He's a complex character that changes. It was an interesting process. I didn't have totally preconceived notions but that's the cool part of it—you take an actor who you respect and see what he comes up with and you talk it out and you come up with something.

I was totally open for anybody to go off and put in what he wanted. I'm not a "You must say it word-for-word" person. Actually the way George worked was he actually read every screen direction I wrote in the script—which even I didn't pay attention to anymore. When we were editing, I looked at him in the car and he was doing what I said at every moment with every line. He worked that way. Liz, played by Elizabeth Ledo, didn't. In the beginning, it was good that we had rehearsals because she wasn't giving him his cues, and he needed his cues. She was giving the gist of the scene, and he was giving a word-for-word performance and working off her cues. I remember the first thing we did was just a disaster, and I was thinking, "I don't know what I'm doing." But she came around at the twenty-fourth hour—she kicked ass.

Mark Yoder went through his agent's files and pulled a bunch of headshots. We went through the headshots and picked who looked right physically. The funny part was that George was not one of my picks—his headshot didn't look like him. Headshots mean nothing. I've never believed in them. But when I looked at George I almost passed him up in the headshots, and I know the headshots mean nothing. But I just thought, "I don't think he's right at all." But he came in more prepared than anybody. He came in with these teeth saying, "I can take them out or put them in. I think they look better if they're out." He said, "I'm growing my beard and my hair and it'll be much longer by August when you said you were going to shoot this." He knew everything. And then his monologue just blew us away and there was no way it was going to be anybody else. It helps when you have an actor who is doing most of the work—it was amazing how much of the prep work he did. He was so professional I was just blown away.

Chad Etchison

It wouldn't have been the film that it was without my DP, Jim Hunter. Look at all the great directors: David Lynch had Frederick Elmes; Alfred Hitchcock had Robert Burks, who won an Oscar for *To Catch a Thief,* and he shot almost all of his films. If you go down the line you'll find that most of the great directors found somebody that they liked to work with. And there's a good reason for that—they made the director look good.

That category we took very seriously and Jim definitely fulfilled that position and beyond. For one thing he could draw, and I think that storyboarding is the greatest thing you can do. I had to storyboard this film. I had already storyboarded the whole film on stick figures, but it was ridiculous—it looked terrible. So Jim said he could draw. We talked

The Initiate's Director of Photography Jim Hunter helms the camera at the reunion scene.

© 2000 Etch-Me Films. Photo by P. Daniel Maughon.

to a couple of storyboard artists and one guy ended up doing some storyboards for us. But most of the boards that we shot, Jim actually drew. So not only did he shoot the film, not only did he assemble the crew, but he drew. I would sit there and tell him what I wanted, and he would sit there and draw. He got to the point where he could knock out a scene—we'd do quick thumbnail sketches, and the next day he'd come back with a finished thing. We probably storyboarded 70 percent of the film in preproduction. The additional 30 percent he was having to do after a long day of shooting. He would keep me from making mistakes I would have made as a rookie filmmaker—he made me look more advanced than I really was.

We did extensive film tests on the 48 and the 93. At first we thought we had to do the 93. Jim did focus tests—he tested the cameras and the lenses at different increments and also tested the stock. Basically, we were looking for density—rich blacks and nice contrast. I think the reason Jim picked the 48 is because of the blowup factor. The 48 is so thick it blows up really nicely. The 93 is great for direct-to-video. But the 48 is just so much stronger especially for blowup, so we really put a lot of thought into the stock.

I originally thought I would write a script to see if I could write a script—that's how it all started. And then I thought, "You know what, nobody's ever going to buy this—realistically nobody gives a damn about my script." On paper it was probably not the most exciting script you ever read in your life and it may not fit the demographics of eighteen- to thirty-five-year-olds. Or it wasn't *Slacker* enough or it wasn't big time enough or who knows what. And I said, "Screw it. I'm not gonna sit around and wait." All they're going to say is, "Hey, great first try. Write another one and give us a call. Don't call us. We'll call you." So I decided to produce it myself and just cut through all that and hope that it would work out.

This was my first script, too. I had started and stopped two or three scripts, and I thought I'd never finish one. The formatting is really hard if you don't know how to type. And I didn't know how to type and the formatting was killing me. I'd come up with an idea that was OK, and I'd get ten pages into it and I'd think, "What do I do now?" It was hard to get from point A to point B. But something about this story was different. I got this story. I got past the formatting problems—I formatted it perfectly. Once I got myself in the real parameters of the format, I just started flying through it. And I made it connect. I remember over the holiday I took a break. I took two weeks off where I didn't write anything and then I just finished it right up in January/February and then we started shooting it in October.

I tried to do a basic outline of the script, but I got bored with doing that, and I just started writing it. Everybody told me you have to outline the script. I broke a lot of rules with the screenplay as far as things you're supposed to do ahead of time. I just started writing it. There are certain things you're supposed to do—the first ten pages are supposed to be pretty significant, and then you have plot points—so I was trying to do that stuff and make it three acts. I just started writing it and tried to keep it going—ending one scene and leading into the next scene. I read a couple things by screenwriters who said it would take on a life of its own and that you just sort of have to go with it. That's what I was trying to do.

I was also trying to have recurring things run through it—subtle things. You'll notice in the great films there will be a major theme. In *Blue Velvet*—which is about violent relationships and sadomasochism and this underworld that exists—you have this beautiful exterior of this nice house in this nice neighborhood. But lurking underneath, it's like I could be going down in my basement—I could be some kind of freak. There's this underworld that's under everything. He suggests that right away by the camera going underground and suddenly you see these beetles attacking each other. You know immediately. I wanted to have things like that.

So it took me about four months to write the script. I did three drafts of the script and in between the third and fourth draft, a professional story editor came in and went through page by page and painstakingly broke up some scenes. It made it much snappier and

65

more detective-ish. But I got to do everything that was in the script. I didn't have to change the story. We shot it just like I wrote it. I got to do it like I wanted to do it.

Then after I wrote the script I got with Jim in April and we started story-boarding in June—June, July, and August. All together, it was about six months of preproduction. The storyboarding was very extensive. We did lighting diagrams, and we scouted locations. One of the steps I skipped as a director was the projecting, which I thought about doing, but I ran out of time. Basically, you go to a location and measure the room you're shooting in. You can figure out exactly where everything is going to be, what focal lengths you're going to use, and how far the talent is going to be from the lens. You can have the whole thing planned out from top to bottom. But I don't know who can do that in that short a time. I felt storyboarding was crucial. What's so great about storyboarding is that now that I'm editing, the boards come back out again. It's our map. And without storyboards I would have been nothing. I would forget what I had planned to do, and I would freak out and be on the set and be lost. But I'd look at the storyboards and say, "Good. Everything's OK. We've got this figured out." Without storyboards, you forget so quickly.

It's so fun when you're in that preproduction stage. You're just thinking up shots. And you're composing things, and you say, "I want this to do this. Jim, can we do this? Oh yes, we can make that happen." Later, when you're shooting the film, you say, "Remember that thing you wanted to have happen? Well, it's going to take this dolly and these special spotlights. And it'll take three days to do ten seconds of dialogue." I asked, "Jim, can we make it rain in this house scene with this fireplace?" And Jim said, "Oh yeah, man, that'll be so great." And then we got there and there were three guys on the roof dropping hoses down, and the whole house was tented in black. It looked like they were bombing a house for asbestos or something. It was a sunny day and it was raining inside. There were flicker boxes that kept going off that were supposed to be the fireplaces and I thought, "Why did I even . . . ? I should have done a movie with a bunch of master shots." Now that it's done, it's so fabulous, but when you're doing it. . . .

If you've done a short and you tried all those things, you would have known when you made your feature. Next time I'll probably be really scared about doing anything. But that could be a bad thing, too, because I was so naive I was just shooting the works not knowing it was going to take so long. We spent seven days in one location and we probably got three pages. You're supposed to average two pages a day. It was tough. And we had a very small crew. It was a small group of very dedicated people. If it hadn't been for them—you know, it's without you I'm nothing.

Jim got the whole crew together. He knew who would do it for less and he wanted all young people. The idea was to have everybody be a step above what they were used to doing so that they would get a chance, which is real typical from what I understand. Because I was a step above what I had ever done. Jim, as much experience as he had, had never shot a feature, so it was a first time for him, too. So the whole idea was to find young people who were really into it and that could afford to work for less and that would do it as a commitment to the art.

I did an open casting call, and I found the lead girl and the character Harlan through that. About one hundred people showed up; I only found two people out of one hundred. I wouldn't really recommend a big casting call unless you were advertising in the right markets. I took out an ad in the *Creative Loafing* and it attracted people who were not really usable—they were more like an extra crowd. I cast a guy that I've known for a long time, and the rest of the people came from word of mouth from the people I was beginning to cast. I cast myself. And there was a lot of nonacting talent in the film that did a really good job, which was interesting. I don't know how much of that I would do again because it's tough. That was another area of first-time stuff that you would never know from watching the film. These people did an amazing job.

5

The Shoot—
The Vast Picture Show

There comes a time in every film's genesis when you have to stop talking about it and start shooting it. And therein lies the crux: As intimidating and overwhelming as making a movie is, it is more exhilarating than imagination or words can convey. Filmmaking is both beauty and beast.

Once that first frame is indelibly etched with your design, the magic begins. And so does the madness. You stand center-ring amidst a circus of choreographed performances and you hold fast to your vision. But not so fast that you can't adapt to the hurdles that are inevitably erected in your path. Through it all you take your vitamins, juggle the unexpected, and direct all the players to their grand finale.

The good news—and curiously, the bad news—is that shoots are brief in comparison with the other stages in a film's life. The shorts and features presented here were shot for one week all the way up to fifty-nine days. Their tribulations, lessons, and achievements, though concentrated in time, amassed a world of experience.

Whip Hubley as Jason Schuyler in *Driven*.

Michael Shoob

We shot in 35mm because we wanted the film to look as good as it could be. In fact, at the screening at Paramount, a well-known studio production manager estimated that the film cost $3–$4 million, saying that he figured it would be more, but he knew that the actors probably worked for scale. We wanted the film to look like a picture three or four times its cost, and if you see it on a big screen, it certainly gives that impression.

We shot for about thirty-five days and two pickup weeks during post-production. So, there was a great deal of shooting. We were a SAG film— we paid all of the actors and there were over thirty speaking parts.

We shot a scene outside a liquor store in Pacoima—heavy gang territory. My production manager felt himself to be an authority on dealing with gangs, and decided that the way to soften our presence there was to buy beer for the guy he figured was the leader. The guy got drunk, and there was a skirmish between gang members in front of our crew. Some threats were made against us (which Bob Logan heard in Spanish), and I decided, against the judgment of the UPM (Unit Production Manager),

Director of Photography Joseph Mealey lies on the hood of a car to shoot the airport scene.

to call in some cops. When the police arrived, the gang members seemed to lose interest. Then I could think about directing the scene and not whether I would be responsible for someone on our crew getting hurt.

I'm probably blanking on numbers of other funny or ironic incidents, and probably I'm not the best one to ask. Firing the transportation guy because he wanted to save money by not putting gas in the generator makes me so damned livid that I can't laugh . . .

One of the principal issues in shooting the film was that we were shooting much of the film in a moving car. How could that be made compelling? How had it been done in previous cab movies like *Night on Earth*? We settled on a camera truck towing a flatbed trailer where the "buck," or shell of the cab, would be situated. The camera operators and I sat on the trailer while key crew rode on the camera truck. We hoped for greater flexibility with this setup than we ultimately got. It just took too long to move the equipment around to allow for elaborate camera movement on the flatbed. Also, the background and available light issues forced us to spring for a second camera, which we hadn't anticipated.

And I didn't realize how much I would be at the mercy of mediocre or just plain bad camera-truck drivers. They had to be able to move the rig to the curb on a second's notice. They had to do all kinds of improvisations, and it wasn't easy. After some difficulty with a few drivers, I finally decided to get a guy who had a supposedly terrific reputation. Unfortunately, his wife had just dumped him. He was unable to sleep. So he arrived on the job half dead, and to stay awake he had to sing along with bad Neil Diamond music on the radio. Unfortunately, I had to hear those songs in my headphones in order to give him direction.

In the midst of this, I should add that the actors (and I had over thirty speaking parts) were virtually faultless. I rarely had an actor go up on a line or arrive unprepared. The folks we cast were glad to be there, and they handled themselves very well.

For an independent film, I should again emphasize that you can do amazing things and overcome amazing obstacles if you have a terrific group—the producer, Daniel Linck, was tireless and cared deeply about making a good movie. The UPM, Bill Burke, was willing to throw himself into a myriad of difficult decisions, and he fought through exhaustion and two ADs who virtually collapsed to make the picture go. The coproducer, Jane Valentine, was a veteran of movies-of-the-week, and she seemed to have a practical solution for a number of difficult issues. The list goes on and on. Friends like Bob Logan showed up and pulled a whole shift as an assistant director when my ADs went down. In fact, I can recount crazy situation after crazy situation. But it's a tribute to the people who cared and stood in there for the film that we did as well as we did, even though they weren't making a fortune.

Jennifer Farmer

We were very lucky on both films in that we did not have rain—I guess that's why they make movies in southern California, because of the good weather. *Pumpkin Man* was a nine-day shoot. When you're shooting a forty-four page script in nine days that's about five pages a day. When you include company moves and moving to new locations, that's a wing and a prayer. But that's what low-budget filmmaking is all about. You can do it if you really plan it out well. We broke it up into four to five days at first and then four days with a two-week break in between where we all got more money, got more rest, and got reorganized a little bit.

Naturally Native was an eighteen-day shoot. Shooting a feature film in eighteen days means you're shooting seven to eight pages a day. I remember being very frightened at the beginning that that was a lot because that left no margin of error. But I was also committed to not burning out my crew on either one. There needs to be a humanity and a joy and a celebration in what we're doing because the work is so very hard. So we had fourteen-hour days on both shows, and the crew knew to expect that. An experienced crew knows that. So it was a brief, yet full-on schedule.

Scheduling was alarmingly smooth in *Pumpkin Man* and *Naturally Native* as well. Nothing really caused us to need to extend things. Again, I think that's because of the strong preproduction.

Whenever you're shooting any particular shot, any particular setup and particular location, there's always going to be the need for flexibility—let's try it over here, let's try it over there. If the AD comes to me and says we are running out of time, there's got to be a backup plan in the back of my head for how we can combine shots, how we can change the blocking a little bit so we can accomplish what we need to accomplish and get it done in fewer shots. As I'm shooting, I'm editing in my head. It's very important to know that you're going to be in a close-up on this person for that line and in a close-up on that person for that line and you'll need to be in a two-shot for the exchange here. You'll need to know emotionally and psychologically why it's a good idea to do all those things.

So that's how I plan my shots—to know where I want to be and why. That way you don't have to spend a lot of time and money and film and cost of developing in having everything covered six ways from Sunday. You can't do that. You don't have the luxury of time and money to do that, so you really need to know what you're talking about when you go in. I watch big-budget movies and I'm jealous of the extra shots and the

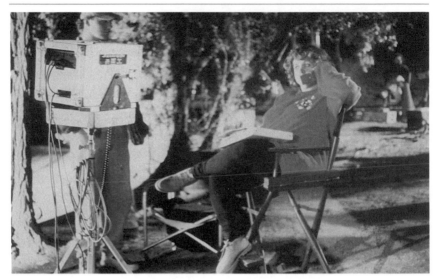

Jennifer Wynne Farmer, director and producer, on the phone during the filming of *Pumpkin Man*. © Pumpkin Pictures LLC.

extra time that they have to do these things, but because we are story-telling there is a way to get in the scene, tell the story, tell it nicely, and get out.

I'm a big fan of big "one masters," as they call them—having a scene, if it's a short enough scene, take place in one take or in one shot with-out having a lot of coverage. In *Naturally Native* we had a seven and two-eighths-page scene, the purpose of which was to show the lead character, Vicki, living a very frantic life and being very frantic. People are coming and going out of her life, and her family is very demanding—one person wants this thing, another person wants another—and at the end of that she breaks down and goes to take a drink of wine, which is something she vowed she wouldn't do. Now, alcoholism is a very touchy subject with Native Americans, and I'm trying to break stereotypes with this film. I thought if I could motivate the audience to be as exhausted at the end of that scene as Vicki was, they would be a little more understand-ing when she goes to take the wine, and they wouldn't think, "Oh there's just an Indian who's drinking too much."

When you're using short ends on the free film that you've been given in low-budget filmmaking, you can't plan a scene for more than about four minutes, and I needed seven minutes, so I broke the scene. We had it cut in a couple of places, but it really does work. At the end of the scene you are exhausted with Vicki, and there is an understanding of why she did what she did. Hitchcock would do that a lot—very short takes.

And the same way in *Pumpkin Man*. I have a 360-degree shot where the legend of Sam Hain—kind of the crux of the film—is being told by one of the characters, and he walks around the kids in a circle sort of campfire style, telling this spooky Halloween story about the guy that lives on the edge of town. I wanted the audience to feel the tension of all this, and when you cut and go to a different angle or different shot there's a psychological rhythm or psychological breathing that happens. I wanted the suspense created in the same way that Hitchcock created it so many times and so well. So we had that 360-degree shot go around twice and by the end of it something spooky comes to break the scene and it's a very good effective moment.

I think any director who tells you that there's nothing they would do differently, no tricks that they've learned, is either absolutely lying or absolutely foolish. Any time you have a filmmaking experience there are things you would do differently—usually under the category of having more time and more money. Sometimes it's all about having experience and wisdom from the work that you've done. That's why they give out lifetime achievement awards to people who are over a certain age. It takes a lifetime to receive those achievement awards because of all the things that they've learned. Absolutely there are things to learn—there are things to do differently next time. There were no disasters. There was nothing that I felt, "Oh my gosh, I wish I'd never done that." I believe if they were right decisions at the time then even in hindsight they will hold. I enjoyed the learning process of it, but I felt I was well prepared.

Any time you have a filmmaking experience, everybody's learning something. If they're not, things can get out of balance. And so the key, particularly to a first-time director/producer, is to have as many experienced, well-seasoned crew members, particularly in the key departments, as you can. Things are going to go a lot more smoothly.

We would have loved to have more time on both films, but according to the editors we were not missing any shots, any scenes, or anything crucial at any time. It's something of a debate.

We ran over budget on both films, but in a way that we took as a tumble and not as a disaster, and we were able to get more funds. I went back to my friends and family and said, "We've made it this far. We've got a good film. This'll make a great film. What do you say?" It's like being halfway through labor—you've gone this far you might as well complete the job. We were able to get more funding. On *Naturally Native* Valerie Red Horse found that she needed additional funds to finish the film and was able to find them personally in the equity of her home. Again, when you can see the ribbon of the finish line at the end of the race, there's no reason to give up and stop, because then you lose all the money.

We followed the script very much. We might change a word here or there, but I don't want to turn on the camera until the script is good, so we followed it very well. There were little moments here and there when the actors or the DP suggested changes, but they were never out of the lines of the story line.

Because we didn't do major script changes, the morale was good. The people from *Pumpkin Man* still call me every week or so to tell me what a delightful, wonderful, enjoyable, terrific, professional experience it was for them and to ask when we will be doing another one. And I respond to them very vividly, "I hope it's very soon." People from *Naturally Native*—same thing. People called up and said this touched their life, this changed their life, this was a filmmaking experience unlike any they had ever had. Perhaps they were first-time PAs (production assistants), or perhaps they were very seasoned members and they had been in Hollywood for a very long time. I was very honored to hear that, because that was definitely what I was wanting to create all along. It really is like being in a family. It's very hard to give up after you wrap. Everybody wants to stay in touch. So we do.

Ali Selim

I had three long lunch rehearsals and one full day walk-through at the location with the two main actors. When it came time to shoot we rarely did more than three takes. It got to the point where I felt that I was almost too prepared. There were few questions and no road blocks. We just moved fluidly from shot to shot and no one ever seemed confused or tired. Not a very energetic, creative atmosphere, but very positive—and that is always the most important element.

Also, we had the first six consecutive days of sunshine in Minnesota in three years. Blessed.

During this initial production, we shot all of the neighborhood exteriors, including the nighttime stuff and all of the first floor house interiors. The bedroom and hallway and basement of the old man's house we saved for studio.

We shot all of the bedroom scenes and the basement scenes in a day

Peter Syversten, John Mohs, and Kyle Davies, from *Emperor of the Air*. Photo by Mike Welckle.

on sets that were built from discarded flats from a local studio. The second day of this weekend was a night during which we shot all the flashback night stuff—the evacuation, the boy climbing the tree, etc. On the third day of the weekend, we took my car, the DP, the gaffer, the AC, and the actress who played the man's wife to Wisconsin. We shot three scenes by the river and fished for trout the rest of the afternoon. The next day we had a wrap party and everyone came. Happy.

We shot the entire film on 35mm Arriflex cameras—largely because we had a freezer full of 35mm film left over from commercials. It made it cheaper to shoot on 35mm than to sell the stock we had and buy new 16mm stock. The cameras were a little bit more, but not so much more that 16mm made financial sense. Besides, with 35mm we could shoot 1:1.85 and make it look like a real movie. Except for one shot, we shot the entire film with an 18mm lens. We just wanted to try to design the film around what is essentially a singular point of view, and 35mm could better capture this subtlety.

Traci Carroll

The first day on the set Jim Hunter laid all the lights and the grip equipment out and said, "This is a junior, this is a tweenie, this is a C-stand, this is a stinger. Everybody knows this so that when I ask for it, you'll know what it is." So that's how we all—everybody that worked on the film—learned from Jim right there on the set as we did it.

The night before we started shooting I felt like we had everything under control and that we knew what was going on—everything was going to work like clockwork. Then when I got on set, Jim said I had the deer-caught-in-headlights look. I had no idea what I was doing at all. My mind went blank and I couldn't picture any of it in my head and I couldn't remember what came next in the script and it was horrible. Tripp, who has actually directed his own script but works in the film industry as a grip, was telling me the lines for the characters because we'd had fifteen takes of it and I couldn't remember what they were. After that first day I was ready to throw in the towel and call it quits. I was so dis-

Brian Turner as Guy in *Five O'clock Shadow.*

couraged; I thought it was so hard. It was so difficult to manage. But it got easier from there. I called Jim and said, "I can't believe this. It's so hard." And he said, "Don't worry, everything will be fine."

I was really stressed out with how slow it was going and how much we had left to do. I thought, "There's no way we're going to be able to finish this film." So I cut the script down to where I felt there was a realistic way to finish the film. That worked to our advantage because the final film is twenty minutes whereas our finished film might have been closer to forty had we left it intact. I have found since I have been entering festivals that nobody's interested in a film between thirty and sixty minutes because it's too long to be a short and too short to be a feature. They don't know how to program it. I know a lot of people out there with forty-five-minute films that don't get into any festivals because they have a weird length film. Of course we didn't know that when we started out, but it worked out to our advantage. A lot of festivals take under thirty; some take under twenty, which ours just barely qualifies for; then there're some festivals that take under ten so we're not eligible.

We broke shooting up into weekends in October, November, and

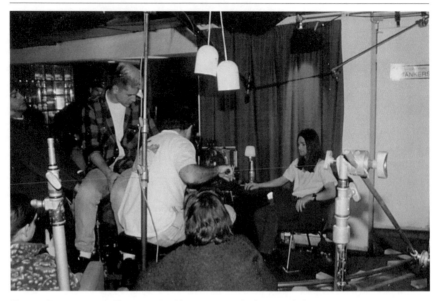

First Assistant Camera Operator, David McLean, and Director of Photography, Jim Hunter, set up a shot with actor Brian Turner.

December of 1995. And everything went really smoothly the first three weekends that we did it. We coordinated the crew so that everybody could be off for the weekend. We were shooting in a bar that was open on Saturday nights. So we had to go in really early, like seven o'clock in the morning, and set everything up and start shooting and be wrapped out of there by eight o'clock that evening so they could come in. And they had posters and stuff up on their mirrors and trinkety things out on their counters and all this stuff we had to take down and shoot around, then put it back exactly the way it was before. Then it would be open for business and everything would be totally trashed—there would be food on the floor and beer bottles everywhere. So then, we had to come in on Sunday and clean up—mop the floors and sweep and rearrange the furniture. So we spent a lot of our shooting time re-arranging the location. We realize now that the better way to do it is just to say, "We need to shoot in your bar five days in a row. Can we just close it and we'll pay you some money rather than trying to shoot around your business schedule?" We could have easily gotten all of the stuff shot in four days instead of six had we gotten full access to the area where we could leave all the equipment there. We didn't know any better—Jim tried to tell us.

We had three people in the cast: Brian who was the lead character, Lauri who was the femme fatale, and Kristi Lindstrom who was our dancer, and she was just there for one day—she was sort of filler. And we had a number of extras. It's really difficult to work with extras, especially if they've never been on-set before. They don't know what they're doing; they don't understand why it takes so long; they get impatient; they want to leave after we've already shot with them in one direction. We probably had ten to fifteen extras that we were working with in the bar.

Once we got to the second location we were dealing with, which was Brian's apartment, it was great because the only actors we were dealing with were Brian and Lauri. Brian was in a lot more stuff than Lauri, so we only had to schedule her for one weekend. The pivotal scene in the film is this love scene, and there's no chemistry between Brian and Lauri at all. We probably spent $5,000 one weekend with scaffolding and lights and everything to shoot this stuff in the bedroom, and it was horrible. It was terrible—every time I saw it I would just laugh because it was so pathetically bad. She looked like she was dead, and Brian would just cringe. He said, "We're screwed. We don't have a movie now." It wasn't a scene we could just not have in the film. We had to figure out a way to fix it. We decided that we were going to have to get a body double.

What worked out for us is that in the beginning Lauri didn't want to dye her hair black for this character. She had sort of medium-brown hair with some blonde highlights. And we really felt like the character needed to have black hair, so we bought a wig for her. So in the end it worked out because when we had to get the body double for her, Brian's girl-friend Jennifer said she would shoot the additional love scenes—the additional shots. She was the same coloring but she had this mass of curly dark hair, so we put the wig on her and it was amazing just how much the wig made it seem like she was Lauri. It was still really difficult because their faces are really different and they don't look alike. How do you have a love scene if you never see her face? We only had two shots with Lauri that we could use. We had a shot of them in front of the window at the very beginning, and we had this overhead, wide shot of them in bed. All the close-ups were unusable, so now we had to shoot close-ups with a completely different person.

Another problem was we didn't have another $5,000 to spend, so we were trying to figure out how to match these really brilliant bright HMI lights to something that was a lot cheaper. So I painstakingly story-boarded everything out as sort of proof that we didn't have to show the windows, that we didn't have to show her face, that we could sort of hide her behind Brian and only show part of her jawline or whatever. I told Jim, "OK, these are the shots and all we have to do is make a tungsten lamp look like an HMI lamp." Jim said, "It can't be done." But I told him, "I know you can do it because you're really good."

Because we had this venetian-blind shadow on the wall, we ended up taking the venetian blinds and putting them on a C-stand. We pushed the bed into the middle of the room so the C-stand could be next to the bed. And then we got a junior, which is just a big tungsten lamp—basically the light is yellow instead of blue—and we put a ton of blue gels on it which made the light blue. It also meant we had to shoot the film with a really wide aperture, which meant that the depth of field was really shallow, which meant that our camera operator had to be absolutely on the money every time he pulled focus to make sure nothing went soft. Now that it's edited and cut together, you cannot tell the difference between the two girls. Jennifer cannot even tell the difference between her and Lauri. And the lighting matches beautifully. Jim did such a fabulous job matching everything, and John kept everything totally in focus. I felt like that was my real triumph as a director, to solve that particular problem and get everybody to buy into it so that we could do it. We maybe spent $1,500 that weekend, instead of $5,000 getting these great shots that really worked. I feel like that is my big victory—I figured out a way to make that work.

The crew was great. They were so willing to learn; they wanted to learn and wanted to be there, even for free. It was just wonderful. We felt like we needed a big crew, but we ended up with seven people who worked constantly. There was me and Jim and Brian, who helped with the setups as well as actually being in the film. Plus we had our assistant camera operator, the second AC who did the slates, somebody who was doing continuity, and Phil Scroggs. Phil was the best—he did everything. Phil was in our credits seven or eight times. He was three or four extra characters—we would put different makeup on him or only show part of him. Phil played extras, did lunches for us, and ran errands for us—Phil did everything. We almost felt like Phil was the fourth partner in the film—there was me and Brian who paid for it and Jim who lent his expertise, and then there was Phil who helped us with everything else. He was really awesome, and I feel in so many ways we could not have done the film without Phil.

I remember the first day on the set I had no idea what I was doing. But we shot for twelve days, and by the last day I felt like I could go out and do a feature film and know what I was doing. Of course, finding someone like Jim Hunter who will teach you hands-on, one-on-one is like finding a needle in a haystack—there's not many people like him who would do that. I think he was willing to take a chance on us because he realized that Brian and I were the type of people who had the money to put into it, were really dedicated to finishing it, and weren't going to wimp out when it started to get too expensive or too hard. So this film was my initiation into filmmaking.

David Zeiger

Displaced was mainly shot on 16mm film, but we reached a point where we knew we wanted to do a lot of extensive interviews on camera, so that's when we started using video. We couldn't do that on film—it was just too expensive a proposition. So we took the Hi-8 camera and set up all our interviews—all with a white backdrop behind everyone so everyone was in the exact same context—and we made the interviews black

Filmmaker David Zeiger captures a moment between his son, Danny, and Mary Ellen Wiggins. © 1998 Displaced LLC. Photo by Ruth Leitman.

and white. Actually, they're sepia-toned so they look like film—they don't look like video. It worked really well because people were surprised we shot that on video. We were able to shoot sixteen to eighteen hours of interviews that we would not otherwise, and those interviews are pretty central.

Then when I started working on *The Band* I knew I'd have to shoot that on video because you just can't shoot that kind of work with film anymore. For *The Band* I had to have the camera rolling all the time.

I didn't have enough fear when I started. I tend to just go in and do it. The times when I had some fears and problems were after shooting something and realizing I had screwed up because I didn't pay attention to certain things. The big thing is audio. I went into it with the same attitude that I did with my still photography—just get in there and do it. I think that's the right attitude. I'm glad I have that attitude because you get a lot more that way. I've learned kind of painfully over time that you've got to pay attention to the technical stuff.

Greg Pratt from *The Band.* ©1998
Displaced LLC. Photo by Mike Kandrach.

The thing that documentary filmmakers, particularly, and new independent filmmakers, generally, ignore is audio. That's the thing that you ignore, and that's the thing that will kill your film faster than anything else. If you have bad-quality film, you can work on it and fix it. If you have bad-quality audio, you're screwed. There's a lot of technology out there that costs a lot of money that can work on it and improve it, but it can't perform miracles. I learned a lot of this in the course of doing *The Band* because audio was such a nightmare. High school is a noisy world and to get isolated stuff is very hard. I didn't want to have people wired. Because I didn't want to see a lavalier microphone, we lost a lot of stuff that we could have had otherwise, but in this case I think it was right because I didn't want to have that feeling.

Chris Blasingame

Yes, I felt like we needed more time, but I was ready to shoot. I needed more money. I needed a lot of things, but I was ready to go. We shot on

85

(From left) Video Assistant Mike Hartigan, Director of Photography Therese Sherman, and Dolly Grip Doc Pedrolle set up the shot. Photo by Tim Sabo.

super-16mm. We had five shoot days—Wednesday through Sunday. But then I went back and picked up stuff on three different pick-up days, and I think I need one more.

I turned over the cinematography job to Therese Sherman who was hired to be key grip, and it was her camera package. I saw her reel, and I thought it was fair for me to be abandoning this position because I was going to be so busy and she was totally capable—more than capable. I liked her stuff. So I asked her, "Hey would you like to do this?" And it worked out well.

There are a lot of things I would do over again, but before I did them I knew that. For one, we had the hardest day of shooting—the camera car day—the first day, and nobody was gelling. To start, you basically want to have some blow-off scenes so that everybody communicates and the crew starts to get used to each other. But we started with the hardest day. Nobody there had worked with a camera car before—at least I don't think anybody had. So it was a new experience for us. We were kind of

Sound Mixer Bill Jenkins (on right) confers with George Wilson as he and co-star Elizabeth Ledo prepare for the next shot. Photo by Tim Sabo.

savoring the opportunity, but we didn't get all the shots we needed. And there was one major oversight with that. We could have planned it to death but until we got on the set and did it we were not going to know all the ins and outs.

The camera car is as big as a semi. And we got to this road that we had timed in preproduction with our location scouts that we could get three-minute takes—which would have been fine. I never used a camera car before and I pictured it as the size of a tow truck that could turn around at the end of the road and go back. But it was really the size of a semi, and we took big twenty-minute loops every time we had to do a take. The problems we had then were—we didn't totally utilize the camera car then—we should have been pumping HMIs through the windows to keep the lighting consistent. But we didn't do it because we were on half-thinking mode. Me included.

You always think you need to do more, but at some point experience needs to take over. I was comfortably prepared for everything, but there were some things I would never have been able to prepare for. I could have probably gone and seen the camera car, taken a measurement, tried to find a semi down there, and tried to make the turn to see if it would have turned around, but I didn't do that. We could have gone crazy with being prepared, but I think we were fine.

One of the most frustrating things—and this is an example of not gelling totally—is scene twelve when Roadrunner and Lizard are talking and trading off lines. Somebody said, "They're talking over each other's lines," like that was the worst thing in the world for editing, and I had a million things on my mind, and I was somewhere else in the car. And they said, "They can't do that." I asked, "Why can't they do that?" They said, "You can't edit." So I mistakenly gave the direction to not talk over each other's lines. That was the worst mistake I made. I wasn't thinking when I said that. I was thinking we'd have cutaways and stuff to cover it, but we didn't, so we have one scene with them trading off lines. One would stop, then the other one would go. It's awful. I hate it. But those are the problems you come up with.

Everything seemed to work out, but there were really frustrating things, like the AD and I both took the time to break down the script and make lists of props. Yet the people who were supposed to be responsible for that didn't read it. So there was an incident when we told the arms guy that we needed this kind of fire, but we needed a similar dummy gun as a prop. Nobody got the gun. Nobody took responsibility for getting the gun or making sure there was a gun. So we used four different guns and we did our best to disguise them, but there are four different guns, and it's supposed to be one gun. And that comes from not having a real prop person.

We were lacking in the prop department, but that was a problem I guess that preproduction was not going to help anyway—there was really nobody to do it. It's sort of annoying because we were giving a PA an opportunity to move up and he just didn't do it. Even if you don't know what you're doing, ask questions. But apparently the PA was having problems with certain people on the production telling him what to do.

(From left) AD Christina Varotsis, Director/Producer Chris Blasingame, Coproducer and "Sheriff Earl" Mark Yoder, and Script Supervisor Renata Pasmanik discuss coverage of the car sequence. Photo by Tim Sabo.

Here's a great roll-with-the-punches story. It took three tries to get a car. First we had selected a 1964 Cadillac and I went down with cash to buy it, but they had already sold it that day. This was three weeks before the shoot. Then we thought we could get a 1963 Buick that wasn't really quite right, but some guy in Chicago was providing it as a favor. I went to go see it, and it was pretty good and would have worked, but it got towed and impounded and nobody knew where it was the day before the shoot—hours before. Steve Barnard, my contact on the location, found this guy who drove into his bar with a 1966 BelAir and I didn't see it. I asked, "Steve, is this the car?" He said, "Yeah this is exactly what you want." Steve had never made a movie before and I don't even think he had read the script—I had just told him about it. But he was right on the money—he couldn't have been more right. The owner was this guy who was excited that we were making a movie—everybody was excited—and he was excited that his car was going to be in the movie. I eventually bought it from him, but at the time he was doing me a favor by renting it really cheaply. So that was hours before the shoot. And the first day of shooting was the car shot. So it's just amazing how you jump blindly and everything sort of falls into place.

I would shoot a lot more. I just like the war of it—it's a big war, and I like being the general. We had thirty people there, but I really saw only six or seven. I saw the grips, the script supervisor, the AD, Mark, and the actors. I know we had people prepping the dime-store set, and there were a lot of other people, but I don't know what they were doing there.

We had a lot of tension because of the food. One of the things you just don't want to do is not feed people. It's stupid, and you've got to feed people and make them feel like people. You can't treat them like crap. I wasn't up for fourteen-hour days—I didn't want to do that. I also don't want to go without a meal for a long time, although I don't think I ate that much the entire week. You've just got to keep people happy—it's just common sense. Initially, only one meal was planned when we were working ten- and twelve-hour days. My parents came down for the last day, and they saw the problems and didn't even know what was going on. And I thought, "Whatever we do today let's not mess up dinner—let's get a nice dinner." It was an hour before wrapping, and we still had no food. So my parents had to run out and get food, and all they could find was pizza. One of my big things I want to do on my next film, *Cold Ground,* where we'll be working hard and working on freezing tundra, is spend money on things like a hot tub or something—silly things that provide comfort and make people happy. It's very important to do that. Even though the responsibility fell elsewhere, I took the crap for it. I didn't want people to think I was being a slave driver, but there's no excuse for it and that's where it falls on me.

There were minor story changes at the time. The story changed after we had to go back and pick up stuff. We had one scene where we shot one shot at night and another at dusk trying to look like night and admittedly they didn't look like each other. So I had to write some insert pages to make the two connect. That was the major script change. Everything else was pretty right on the money.

Chad Etchison

I think that at the beginning of the film there were times that I was doing things because I knew I was supposed to do them as a director, but I didn't exactly understand why. Whereas, if you did a short film first you would see the film all the way from conception to completion after you edited. And there are a lot of things in editing where you think, "Oh that's why we did that." I figured it out about halfway through the shoot. If anybody tells you they're not faking it, they're lying. Half the time you're faking your way through this stuff. You're winging it and hoping that the people that are surrounding you can keep it going. I have to admit that there were several times while shooting that I was completely lost—I had no clue what was going on. We went on a construction site, and we were on a roof, and there was an hour where I didn't even know what town I was in. It was so confusing to me. I have a bad sense of direction, and that's something I'm going to work on before the next film, because as a director, you have to know what's going on—every angle. It's hard to explain, but I got mixed up sometimes.

The great thing about storyboards is it forces you to follow a plan—it forces you to think about what you're going to shoot ahead of time, but it doesn't force you to do it. So if we had all the time that we needed and everything was going well, we'd shoot everything on the storyboards. If I got an idea or Jim got an idea, or if somebody said, "Hey what about . . . ?" then we'd shoot something else. Sometimes we'd throw in an extra shot or two. Sometimes we'd take a shot away—we'd get there and we'd have twenty frames of storyboards and it would be freezing cold and four in the morning, and we would be running out of time and here comes the fuzz—that kind of feeling. So we'd look at this and say, "Do we really need this wide shot? No, we can accomplish this with . . . ," and we'd scratch it. I cannot imagine going on-set and not having storyboards—for me, personally, with my lack of sense of direction. I don't think I could have done that. I wish I had had more storyboarding done.

All the close-ups are really tight—we used a 135, an 85, a 100, and a 50. Those were 35mm and 16mm, so our close-ups are *close-ups,* which I really love. I swiped that from Hitchcock and Lynch, especially from *Lost Highway*. We did it a lot—probably not as much as they did, but we did it a lot.

Locations were hellacious to acquire. Whenever you find a location, you're basically asking people, "Hey can we come in your place of business, shut you down, bring fifty people, and have lights and camera and stuff?" And they say, "Hell no." Here in Atlanta they're much nicer than in California, where they're much more film savvy, and they know the deal, and they're over it, and they know it sucks, and they know it's long hours, and they know it's not glamorous, especially if you're me and don't have any stars. They're over it. Here they're way more interested, and we found that in the rural areas we had more luck.

So we started to film in Columbus where we owned a house that we ended up mortgaging for the film. So we went down there and shot. The whole time we were scrambling for locations. But luckily, we got great deals at Riverwood Studios and at Guy Tuttle's Special Projects. So that's where we did all the sheriff's office stuff and the reunion scene, at Riverwood. That was as close to a big show as we came on the project. If there was one point in my life where I could have hit a fast forward button and gotten through it faster, this would have been it. I remember a lunch break in the middle of the week with my head in my hands thinking, "I can't face it anymore—it's just too much." Unbelievably difficult. Somehow I made it. I'm so much of a better person because of it. It was like boot camp—it was just hell, but it was the greatest thing that ever happened to me. But locations, we didn't secure them, and you're supposed to. But my whole attitude was, if I wait until then, I'll wait until February, so I'm going—I'm going to shoot.

We did not have a cover set. We shot one time outside in the rain. Our location manager did a great job of scrambling to get these locations. We ended up having to go to a town meeting to get the library—they had to vote on it. We were going everywhere for a library and nobody would give us one. Decatur gave us one but it wasn't the right look for the film so we turned it down. Then later, we thought, "We blew it by turning this down." We tried to get it back and they said something like, "No thanks. We went through too much trouble—screw you." We finally found a library in Riverdale that was being shut down—they were transferring to Fulton County and it was all this political hassle but somehow we got in there, and it was perfect. But it was so difficult to secure these locations. For one thing you either have to have a lot of money or you have to have insurance, which we had, but there's just so many things that can go wrong. To secure it and get the timing right, it's just so hard.

It was a SAG film because most of the actors were SAG actors. I had to go through the whole SAG process, which included a mountain of paperwork and was really rough, but it was really great because it brought a real air to the film—it made the film seem like a bigger deal than it was at that point. We got the SAG thing, and because of the SAG thing I've joined the DGA, which is really cool and exciting for me. It's kind of like a vanity thing—you can stick it on the end of your name and it might help. Plus, it has a really good insurance program. So all that stuff helps and makes a difference, but it also makes it harder than if it weren't a SAG thing. You have to follow their rules and it's a lot to do. That's more of that producer-type stuff that I don't enjoy doing.

We did no rehearsal, which I think is a bad thing. I don't know. By not having a rehearsal, everything stayed really raw. Some of the actors were fine without a rehearsal—some of them I wish I'd had some time with, especially since I had a very distinct way I wanted the lines read. That's the number one thing you're not supposed to do as a director is line readings, but that's really hard to resist when you wrote it and you know exactly how every line is supposed to sound. If it starts sounding this other way, you think, "How do I verbalize what I want?" And if I'd had some time rehearsing some of these people I think I could have gotten them closer to where I wanted them to be, but they all did a great job so I have no complaints.

But I do think it would be nice to have some rehearsal time because you could also block each scene. They were amazing. During the last scene at the hotel, we did do some on-the-fly stuff. The last day I had no clue of how I was going to make this thing happen. At the last minute, we figured out some breakaway tables, the trip, and some broken bottles. I staged this whole thing on the fly, and showed them one time. They came running in and did it perfectly on the first take, and then did it two more times identically. It was amazing. I don't know if I was lucky—I think I was lucky because I've heard so many nightmare tales—but everybody was ready to make something happen on this. The crew, the cast—everyone thought, "We're gonna rule this." So it was a trip. I had to block it right then and tell them what to do, and they did it. And a lot of them hadn't acted in a film before. I think a lot of careers were born—we'll see what happens.

The shoot was exactly fifty-nine days. Jim told me it was going to be a sixty-day shoot. I told him we could do it in thirty days but he said, "No—the lowest I'll go is forty-eight days." And I said, "We'll definitely get it done in forty-eight days," and I secretly thought to myself, "We'll get it done way before forty-eight days." But after shooting only three pages that first week, I thought, "We're gonna need ninety days." Somehow we managed to do it in sixty days. I could have used ninety days.

We did cut out some stuff. The script on paper is about an hour and thirty-seven minutes. It's looking like it's going to be a two-hour film with all the stuff cut out. I had all this stuff I wanted to do in the beginning with motorcycles. Once I realized it was going to be impossible to shoot the stunt stuff I had put in there—and it was real minimal, a small wreck—I realized that the whole concept wasn't going to work because ideas come in packages. Once you take out one piece, why leave the other two or three? So I pulled the whole thing out, and that saved our asses because we would have had to shoot it. We also modified the ending to make it more doable—same ending, same content, just a different location. We just cut the bike-shop scene because that all went by the wayside.

It's hard to say what the biggest hell was—money or locations. Money was hell—it was a weekly trauma—how am I going to get the money this

Chad Etchison directs a sequence in the death scene. ©2000 Etch-Me Films. Photo by P. Daniel Maughon.

week? We almost ran out of money several times. It was hellacious—we were paying the crew every week trying to do the right thing by them. Jim had a good point about if you are trying to make a movie for way less, it is your movie, it's not your crew's movie. My crew busted their asses, but I was asking people to do all this work for me for a really low amount of money, and it's a tough thing. And with me being the executive producer and the director, I had to walk this funny line. I had to direct, but I also had to be this producer guy, which I'm miserable at and will never do again. That's the thing I discovered: I have no propensity for producing. Never again. It was only by default that I did it this time, but I don't ever want to do it again. Basically I threw it all on Mary. Mary and Jim did all the coordinating, and they did all the daily UPM stuff. I hate that part of it. I hate the money part of it. That was terrible.

I directed, wrote, acted, and produced. The producing was what sent it over the edge. I had never been in a real film. I had to act in my own film. So I took the role of the bad guy, which is much smaller than the

95

lead—it's a pretty sizable role but it was not so much. Instead of feeling out of control when I acted and directed, I felt even better because acting was my element that I was comfortable in, and I felt like I was right in the middle of it. As a director I felt somewhat isolated sometimes. There's a pro and a con to it. On the days that I was acting I was trying to prepare for that. I ended up giving the directing to other people—I would count on Jim or somebody else. I still directed in the sense that I thought of the shots, but I lost the immediacy and the ability to have an objective view. It's more of a subjective view when you're in the middle of it. You know what you're thinking, but is it working out here? I think you can do it. I had mixed feelings going into it not knowing if it was a good idea. Jim was really against it. But then later he was really excited by what I did acting-wise and I loved acting. I loved it. It is difficult to do it but it is definitely doable. I think if somebody wants to act in their film and direct it, they should definitely not hold themselves back. I think taking the lead is not a great idea because that is too much. What Woody Allen does in his films—sort of flits in and out—I think that's totally doable.

I think a basic for directing is the pyramid—a lot of directors will start out wide and get wide coverage so they've got it, at least. And then they'll begin to go in and get close-ups. There's another view that you get your close-ups first while your actors are fresh. Then there's another view that you do your storyboarding—just plan each shot and don't shoot everything else. One of the things I was wondering was, say you went wide, how quickly can you jump in close? You're out wide and suddenly you're tight—it works if you want it to work—you decide if that's your aesthetic and if that's what you want. But you have to wonder if that's going to confuse the viewer. Is it going to cause the viewer to notice the cut? Because the idea is to keep it clean so they don't even realize what's going on. Will that throw the viewer off? So basically if you storyboard it and you know what it's going to look like, you can make a nice transition. What I wanted to do with the film was to have wide shots to set it up— and that's pretty typical of what everybody does—and medium close-ups for the bulk of the dialogue, and for super important moments really getting lovingly close-up on the actors. Really get that feel of you're right on top. That's what blew me away in *Lost Highway*—you have this huge screen and Patricia Arquette's face is huge. It pulls you in and makes you really get close—you're forced to get close to the characters.

Basically, I would go back to the storyboards to block the scenes. I would say there are patterns I learned about as a director. There's the *I* pattern—if there are two people, it's like an *I*. If there are three people, it's an *A*. If there are four or more, it's like an *L*. Some of the time I would do it on the set, but in the pictures I would say, "OK, we'll have the car here and the guy here, and we'll have the people bending out like an *L*. On the set I'd arrange all the extras and then we'd go back and Jim would look and I'd look and we'd see what looked nice in the frame and go from there. The scenes where there were two people would be all story-boarded—however we mapped it out in the storyboard, we would basically re-create on the set. The storyboards really helped with blocking—it was pretty self-explanatory. With the storyboards you're locked into a certain thing.

I think my film has kind of a slow quality to it, kind of like *L.A. Confidential*, which is kind of like *Chinatown*—it has an unraveling, slow quality. The camera moves a lot in the film, but there are not a lot of quick cuts. The overall theme of the thing is slow until the end, then it starts to spiral out of control. Basically, what I did is I had characters wipe the frame a lot—I had people come into every shot. When the character couldn't move because of the line, we had the camera move. What else did I do movement-wise? I think I basically wanted to shoot it like an old Hollywood movie so the motivation to move would usually be a physical action. If a girl is sitting on the couch, for example, and she wanted to get the drape, that would propel her out of the shot and she would wipe out of the shot. Then we would be stuck maybe on Jack on the couch for a moment and he would go through his moment—that's basically how I would use it.

I had a couple of problems concerning morale—mainly I think it was immaturity. There were a lot of young people there. It's weird because when people came in they were young and hungry and willing to do it for nothing, but once they realized, "Hey, we can get paid," they got in a groove of getting a check every week. Four weeks or three weeks into the thing everybody forgot that it was a little, tiny independent film, and everybody got this weird energy. I remember *Black Dog* was shooting at the same time, and everybody kept talking about it. I think for a while everybody thought they were working on *Black Dog*, but I talked to several people who worked on it, and I found out I was paying comparably. I wasn't paying comparably to a gaffer on *Black Dog*. If that person who was working for me was working on *Black Dog*, they would have been making about the same amount of money, but they wouldn't get to do the great job—they would be doing something like a PA job or something low. So there was a sense that they weren't making much money which is tough, and I understand that completely.

No matter how cool you are with your crew there's definitely an us-against-them mentality that is unavoidable, and everybody talks about everybody else. I did it too, so I didn't care. At the end I had no bad feelings and no animosity. I would say that I would work with 99 percent of the people again. I really would. I had no qualms with any of the people. But there was an ebb and flow—sometimes everybody would be into it. Then it would drop down a little bit and they would say, "We're over this," and, "this sucks," and then the tide would go back up again. But overall I couldn't have asked for a better group of people. I'm not just saying that now that it's over, but I really mean it—I knew that those people were hanging in there.

6

Postproduction—
Four Edits and a Tylenol

When the shooting stops, the directing begins. Again. Post-production is the final opportunity to helm your vision. And the frontier can be an expansive one.

The filmmakers profess that posting was enlightening not only about the nuts and bolts of the process but about finding their story amidst the endless feet of frames. Sometimes characters, storylines, and even the heart of the film reveal themselves only on celluloid.

Physical means abound for editing. Some opt for digital nonlinear processes while others prefer cutting the actual film. But scoring, sweetening, screening—they all play a role no matter which method. From the benefit of their experiences, a portion of the mystery dissolves from the process.

Michael Shoob

I suppose, in some ways, postproduction was one of the most difficult parts of the process for me. It's very similar to the writing process for me, and sometimes walking into the editing room was a little like facing the blank page. The myriad of options are sometimes overwhelming, and then suddenly the lack of options can be equally overwhelming.

I decided, because *Driven* was my first feature and because it was very personal to me, that I wanted plenty of time in postproduction. Also, I wanted to be able to show the rough cut a number of times to get audience feedback. I had made a half-hour short film and edited on an Avid. While I had loved the speed of the Avid, I missed the opportunity to eyeball dailies on a screen. I missed being able to look at the rough cut on a screen. So I decided to cut on film, and I took full advantage of the fact that I could pull the film off of the Kem (a flatbed editing table) and screen for small audiences.

I chose to edit on film primarily because I felt that I wanted to take more time in the postproduction process, and I felt it was important to screen the rough cut a number of times for audiences. Anyone making an independent feature is probably going to have to make a choice between cutting electronically and cutting on film—it's going to be too expensive to use both the Avid and print dailies. Obviously, the Avid is going to get you the opportunity to see lots of options and see them quickly, but I also believe very strongly that if you're making a feature, you better look at the film on the big screen with audiences before you lock the picture for good. The film plays differently on the screen than it does in an editing room, and it feels very different once again with an audience.

If there is plenty of money for post, I would actually suggest some combination of the two—screening dailies on 35mm, then cutting the film electronically. I would then periodically conform the work print and screen for audiences during the editing process. But that's going to be very expensive.

As I mentioned, one of the reasons I chose to edit on film was to have the ability to screen the film anytime I wished. So we screened for groups of twenty or thirty, perhaps six or eight or ten times. Listening to the audience and discussing their response was helpful, although sometimes it makes you a bit crazy. One person loves a scene that someone else hates, etc.

100

It was most useful in discovering what parts of the story we simply did not communicate effectively. If five folks in the audience tell you that they didn't understand why character A was forced to go to location B—you figure that there might be a better or more efficient way of communicating the idea.

We did not, however, do any official test screenings using focus groups. I've been told that this is very helpful to a film, and I confess that I simply haven't had the experience.

I think one of the most difficult elements of the postproduction process for me was to try to understand this new life that was being created. The biggest surprise for me is that the film you write and even the film you're shooting is very different from the film you're making in the editing room.

First, the actors simply bring new colors to the characters—some of them good, some of them not so good (and you can edit them out perhaps), and some just plain different. For example, Dan Roebuck brought a slightly different flavor to his character that I really hadn't written. I now either like it or have come to accept it, but once you're in the editing room and it's a given, you simply live with it and shape the film with the new wrinkle.

Second, perhaps screenwriters (or I as a writer) can create an interesting tapestry and not be really encumbered by length. If the reader loves the characters and the story, he can probably tolerate an extra twenty or thirty pages and never feel it. Even if the script is shorter, a scene may still play long, or a wonderful scene in the script just may not be necessary in the final film. Or, in the case of *Driven,* it might be hurting the balance of the ensemble. Or the rhythm you discover in the editing room simply dictates that numbers of scenes just have to go. Or you give up something you love because it's not having the intended effect on the audience. They just don't get it.

I actually think it's fair to say that you script the film all over again in the editing room. You're obviously reworking it structurally for some of the reasons I've already described. But you're also discovering something both painful and exciting. Maybe the themes you set out to explore aren't really what the film is about. They may be subsets, smaller motifs, but perhaps they are no longer as significant as you believed during writing or even during shooting. Maybe your movie about racism has really become a movie about dreams. Maybe your movie about working-class America is really a movie about masculinity. Obviously, these themes aren't mutually exclusive. But one theme can emerge so much more significantly than another in the postproduction process.

On *Driven,* very broadly, I thought an interesting directorial angle was to think of my guys as "nobodies who become somebodies" in the course of the film. I wanted to vindicate "a bunch of nobodies." But as I continued working in post, maybe even as I was screening the rough cut and trying to learn something from the feedback I was getting, I began to feel that the more critical struggle of these guys was a struggle with the issue of masculinity. What was it to be a man at the end of the twentieth century? If you weren't successful and you were stuck driving a cab, did that mean you were somehow less masculine?

Again, perhaps this change came about because of the actors who were cast—Chad Lowe, for example, plays LeGrand, a cabdriver who is treated as a scapegoat by the other drivers. Chad brought a wonderful innocence to this character, but he also brought a sexuality that another actor wouldn't have brought to the equation.

I guess I really believe that the reason post is so hard is that we're writing and directing and editing these films trying to excavate what we want to say. We think we know, but we don't really know. It's only natural that the truth of what the film is about is buried in the script, in our directorial ideas, in the footage we've shot, and in everything we try to do in the editing room. That's why the process is, by turns, so full of agony and so thrilling.

Jennifer Farmer

If you have a good story, a good film, and a good product to show to people, and if people understand that you know what you are doing and you have focused vision and direction, then you are able to get deals from places. Don't be afraid to ask for deals from big companies. For example Color By DeLuxe, the company that just finished Jim Cameron's *Titanic*, had a little extra jingle in their pocket and were in the mood to be benevolent. Small companies are willing to work with you because they want to get put on the map. And if they believe that you're a company that is going to actually have a film that goes somewhere and does something, that can help put them on the map. Saying please and thank you, being sincere and honest, and not trying to wheel and deal but laying the situation out on the table is always a good way to make deals, and that's what we did.

We used the Lightworks system on *Pumpkin Man* and also on *Naturally Native*. I understand that the Avid system is easier and more editors are proficient on the Avid system, but when the Lightworks system is given to you for free, you go with the Lightworks system. And it worked very well for us.

Everything cut together. There was a scene in *Pumpkin Man* where we needed to take the time to get another shot in there so that it would cut a little more effectively and add to the suspense. So we did go back in and do that as a result of the post decisions, so it worked very well.

In *Pumpkin Man* we needed to create an entire score for the half-hour piece, so I put ads in the trades and was inundated by many composers who were everything from not so experienced to very experienced—all very talented. I received a package from an agent of a woman named Muriel Hamilton. And there was something about it that was special and unique. I can't even tell you what it was, but as I read it I thought, "This is it, this is it, this is it." I listened to many hours of composers' work thinking, "This is not what I'm seeking. This is similar to what I'm seeking." And everybody was suggesting, "You need a Danny Elfman sound if you're doing a Halloween film." And I thought, "Yeah, but every Halloween film that's been done is Danny Elfman." I needed something that was good Halloween music but not necessarily a Danny Elfman rip-off because there's nothing original if people say, "Oh, that sounds like

103

Danny Elfman." So I met with Muriel and we absolutely clicked and developed a wonderful relationship.

I am a classically trained musician. I played piano for eighteen years and majored in jazz piano at North Texas State University. So in what I direct, every scene has a rhythm in the same way that music has a rhythm. In my head I know that music will start up over the opening part of this master shot and music will end here and come in here and cue here and we'll have a musical sting here and there. So as I'm directing I kind of know where the music is going to go. Muriel explained to me that there are so many directors who don't have a clue about where they want the music to start and stop. It was a delightful experience when she and I would get together in her studio and just create together knowing that I wanted major chords here and minor chords here and starting and stopping there. I would never say, "Play it in G here or lower it by a third here or use a clarinet there." We would talk about what instruments we would use, but I would never restrict her process—in the same way that I didn't do that with my actors or my DP or anyone else.

It was an exciting, exhilarating, collaborative effort, so Muriel came over to do *Naturally Native* with us. *Naturally Native* was a little bit different situation in that many performers in the Indian community wanted to be involved in the project because it was an important film. Donna Summer wrote a song for the film and donated it to us for free. And Gloria Estefan gave us "Get on Your Feet" for one of our montages for free. And Rita Coolidge sings "Amazing Grace" in Cherokee during a very poignant turning point in the film. She gave it to us for free. Christofari is a young, new Native American reggae band and they were happy to be on the sound track. So all the songs that we were given for the sound track were donated to us for free. Junie K. Randall is a Native American woman who wrote the end title sequence. All these people came together to be a part of something very important and special. And we have a percentage of the profits going to Walking Shield, which is a nonprofit organization that benefits the Lakota people in South Dakota.

Our characters are Lakota people, so again that was a very special thing about everyone coming together.

The lawyers had a hard time working it out, getting their clients to agree to provide their services for free. They wanted to retract the free part, but we were low budget and we didn't have the money. Everyone believed in the project and believed in what we were doing, so we had an incredible sound track coming together with several record companies taking strong interest in it. So that was a very exciting part of it. Again, for me, being a musician and having a musical background, this was a very important time to put in elements and collaborate in that way. And I can't say enough wonderful things about Muriel Hamilton who has become a beloved friend as a result of this.

Sometimes things that you don't expect will take place in postproduction. We changed the ending of *Naturally Native,* not with any reshooting but with putting different scenes in different places, and it works a lot better that way. A movie will take place in postproduction. I know I said that in preproduction, but the movie really finally takes place in postproduction. Sometimes little things will come to you that are a little different that you didn't plan, but if it works it works, and it can't be argued with.

Ali Selim

We spent five days cutting what we had with the editor, Jim Stranger. We discovered that we had a couple of unforeseen holes or bad transitions. From this realization we created a couple of easy scenes we could shoot in the studio two weeks later that would make sense and hide our omissions.

The next phase of editing took only three days. We plugged in the scenes that we had just shot and spent a day tightening things up. We had a screening for a few friends and decided we were done.

The next phase almost killed me. We tried to put the stars in the sky the old way: optically. After two months of back and forth and great effort on the part of the printer in Chicago, we all agreed that what we had in our minds was very different from what was possible. Since the stars play a major role in the meaning of the film, we decided we had to pursue our mind's eye elsewhere. We counted out the frames that would be necessary to effect and sent them to E-Film in L.A. to have them scanned to disk at $4 a frame-in and $5 a frame-out.

We then begged (for the first time on this production) and convinced Lamb and Co., a local animation house, to give us the necessary Flame time (forty hours at $600 an hour) for nothing. For some reason, they agreed.

When all of this was done, we went to conform the negative for the print. The conforming took about a week because he had difficulty with the calculations. Our first print came to us about a month after that and we discovered that "difficulty with the calculations" was an understatement. Some scenes were cut in half; some were not the right scenes at all. Because of the way frame accurate neg is conformed, we had to go back to the Avid to recut some scenes and all the sound. This took about two days and countless compromises and dollars.

Lesson learned: Cut on the Avid then work print your selected scenes and do the final preconforming cut on a table. I don't care that the Avid sales rep tells you otherwise.

It took about another month to get the second print and though it was all in the correct place, we learned another lesson. If you are effecting a shot but sending it through the scanner-computer-scanner, effect the whole scene, not just a shot. We went through five costly prints trying to match the nighttime shots effected to those not effected. It was shocking purple versus black—a misunderstanding that could only be resolved by tweaking and tweaking.

The sound was nothing. Scored in a day and mixed in a day, and the first sound print was in sync. Go figure.

Traci Carroll

Post probably took nine months if you boiled it down to the time we spent on editing. What was extremely difficult about the editing process was that Brian's schedule at CNN did not at all mesh with my work schedule. He also taught graphic design so we had two to three days a week that we could get together for three to four hours at a time. And then his schedule changed and I had to push my flex hours one way or the other to try and get a little more time with him. At that point I had become a board member at IMAGE and I had certain board meetings and committee meetings there that were taking up my nighttime. It was really difficult for us.

The other thing that was hard was that because we were both living in apartments there was no place to put the flatbed. So IMAGE graciously allowed us to keep our flatbed in part of their space, but then we had to coordinate with them to get a key to the space. And because they were letting us keep it there for free they were renting the machine to other people. So then we had to work around the other people. The other difficult thing about our posting was we shot our film without sound. About two days into shooting we realized the guy doing sound just didn't have it together. We all kind of knew he was smoking pot on the set, and he would just leave the sound running rather than turn it off and on. He was just out of it the whole time. He would be recording sound and we would notice this motorcycle gang down the street and we would ask, "Hey is that on our take?" And he would say, "What motorcycles?" And because it takes so much longer to shoot when you're recording sound versus when you're not—because you're always waiting for that perfect moment of silence in your house when there's not traffic and there's not pipes rattling or whatever—I just decided, "Scrap the sound. We're just not gonna shoot with sound." We had a friend of Jim's come in to shoot one day with our actress, and we recorded sound that day, but after that we shot everything completely without sound. So it went really fast.

Then Brian, Jim, and I got together. We had our work print transferred to video once we had edited the film. We had twenty minutes of silent film transferred to video. We plugged it in, got the microphone, got the sound equipment, and foleyed it over at my house. I actually really enjoyed it. I know Brian told me he hated having to go back and do all of the sound effects. A friend of mine owns a CD library of sound effects, which is worth several thousand dollars, so we used his sound effects for free. We had to get all these effects transferred to mag stock, which is what we used to edit on the flatbed. It would be like, "OK, there's a foot making contact with the floor," and we'd line up that sound effect with the picture, then we'd have to see how much we'd have to add or cut to make the next one line up. And we had to do that with footsteps, sloshing the razor in the water, and all the stuff that we recorded. Then we had to figure out a way to make that match to the picture even though the stuff hadn't been recorded in the same year. So our editing took a long time because of our sound effects process—we edited six full reels of sound effects on the flatbed, where you can only do two at a time, and we had it all mixed down. We had a grid that showed where all the sound effects were on each track and how long they were and what overlapped what. Brian said, "I hope you don't get hit by a bus because I don't know what to do with all this stuff."

We had an original score. Brian and I had gone to school in Athens, Georgia, and the people that he was friends with were in a band in Athens. One of the guys in the band was named Keith Joyner, and he was in a band called the The, and that band is basically the brainchild of this guy named Matt Johnson. Matt does all of his stuff in his studio, and then when he tours, he finds musicians to tour with him to play the instruments. Keith toured with the The, and he met this guy, Andy Kubiszewski, who is in a band now called Stabbing Westward, which is in Atlanta. He's also played with Nine Inch Nails. We knew the type of music that Keith was doing fit with what we were wanting to accomplish with our sound track and the type of film we were doing. So Brian called him and said we were doing this film and we wanted to have this type of sound—this sultry lounge act kind of sound. Keith did a loop and sent it to us on a regular cassette, and he asked, "Are you thinking something like this?" And we thought, "Oh that's really cool."

I honestly can't remember if that loop made it into the final version of our film because after we edited all our film and transferred it to videotape we sent him a VHS copy and he got Andy to work with him on the sound track. So they did an original song with lyrics and then instrumental stuff. We didn't really know what we wanted to do in the way of sound effects for the shaving scene, which was a dream sequence. So we were open to suggestions. They did some nice layered audio effects that weren't music but were other stuff that they thought was cool. It was their own interpretation of what was going on, and we loved it. We added a few more sound effects on top of that, but I feel that what they did was so much better than what we would have done on our own. So that turned out great. The music was really awesome.

Because we didn't know what we were doing, and because they were friends of ours, it didn't occur to us to find out what sort of contractual obligations Keith had with BMI (Broadcast Music, Inc.) and Andy had with ASCAP (American Society of Composers, Authors, and Publishers). A lot of times when a musician has a contract with one of these entities, everything they compose belongs to them rather than the artist. So after we had all our music scored for our film, then we had to get David, a friend who was an entertainment lawyer, to figure out the contract Andy and Brian had with the organizations and determnine whether they were even allowed to do work for hire. It turned out fortunately for us that they were—they themselves didn't even know. So David quickly drew up work-for-hire contracts and had them sign away their music to us so that it would belong to us and not to them or to the organizations. Then we found out that they had sampled music from another band and that band had sampled work from Jean-Paul Sartre. His estate is ironclad and it's very expensive to get permission to use his work. We ended up having Keith send us another track of the music without the voice. But there were lots of little things like that we didn't know. We knew we didn't want to use previously recorded music because then you have to get the rights to that. And we knew it would be cheaper if you had good musician friends to record something that would be perfect for the film.

The other thing that we learned was when you have an actuality—

which is a character singing something or whistling something, or whatever—even though the actuality is being performed by your actor, you have to get the rights to the song. We didn't know this. In this one scene, Brian was whistling circus music. It was relevant to the plot so it couldn't be anything else, and I had no idea what it was called. I had no idea how to find out what it was in order to find out if we could use it at all. So I got on the Internet and found this Web page that actually had audio files on every conceivable circus tune. I found the tune we had used and, fortunately for us, it was in the public domain—it had been created in Czechoslovakia in the 1800s. But it was something we had never thought of.

David Zeiger

There were two hundred hours of raw footage for *The Band*. We shot an awful lot. We shot for the whole school year—nine months. First, I very carefully went through all the tapes in order and made what I called back reels. I dubbed what I thought were potential scenes for the film onto other tapes that had time code. To go through all two hundred hours of that took about six months because I also had to do other work. Then I had all those scenes logged. I think I got about fifty hours. Then I went through it all again and organized it into subject matter. I took all the scenes that I had that I liked of Burt Hudson and Erin and put them together on tapes—same thing for scenes I had of Danny and Mary Ellen. And in the course of that, I created an A-list and a B-list. The A-list was about ten hours. That took another couple months. Then we were ready to start putting it onto the Media 100. We were editing on the Media 100 for about six months.

Most of it I shot on my L1, my Canon Hi-8 camera, and it's interesting because while we were editing, the digital DVC cameras came out and it's kind of unfortunate because if we'd been able to shoot the whole thing on those cameras the quality would have been a whole lot more. . . . One of the things that happened was, knowing that we were shooting it on Hi-8, we knew we were going to have to spend a lot of money on the

Director David Zeiger films Burt Hudson and friend from *The Band*. © 1998 Displaced LLC. Photo by Mike Kandrach.

back end working on the quality of the footage. So we put a lot of money into the online and what's called the tape to tape color correction, which was really worth doing. It was done by a guy at Video Tape Associates, Inc., who does all the color restoration for the films at the Turner archives. He is a real expert at working with color and density. Then we ran it through a film look process. We put a lot of our money into that because we knew that it was just what we had to do to get it ready for broadcast.

We didn't pay people for shooting or working—I did most of the shooting, but then at games James Jernigan shot a lot. We brought Betacams to the games and James shot, I shot, Robert Neely shot, and Greg Pratt did the audio for a lot of that. We put a lot of effort into those events to get them as high quality as possible.

You sort of know where your story is going before you shoot, but you find it as you're shooting as well. I think it's a combination of the two. I did have a general idea that I went into *The Band* with, but a lot of the questions I ran into evolved, like, "Who are the kids who will ultimately be the main characters of the story?" I spent months pursuing the stories of several kids, and they're not in the film. The way I worked is I went into it with a general idea and tried to get as much material on that idea as possible. And then in the editing suite I wasn't looking at the reality out there—I was looking at what I had on film.

Then your whole orientation goes toward the final film itself, and if something doesn't serve the film you can't use it even though it's very interesting in its own right. That's the hardest part about editing. That's why it's important to have an editor work with you and not edit everything yourself. You tend to fall in love with the material or you remember everything else that was going on then or you have a real feel for the footage, but if somebody wasn't there they just aren't going to get it. That happens a lot and you don't really know, and you have to have other eyes looking at it.

It was both during the editing process and also during the filming that I learned a lot about myself. One thing I learned is that I don't like telling people what to do. So I tended to be very hands-offish when we were filming. I'm not real aggressive in interviews—I'm more one to get people talking or get people responding to something, so that's probably why photography suited me. I'm more comfortable when I'm not out there directing even when I'm directing. If I ever make a narrative kind of thing, which I'd love to do sometime, I think I'd be the kind of director that really works with the actors to get them to understand the characters and the dynamics and let them do what they want to do. So I would really need to have actors who are capable of doing that. I've gotten to know a lot of actors, being a theater photographer, and I can see the people who I could work with in the sense that I wouldn't have to get real specific about what they should do and how they should do it because I hate that anyway.

But when I'm editing I get a lot more demanding, I guess, because when I start to see how things are developing I can do everything that I need to do to get things moving in that direction. On the first film, I did all the off-line editing on a simple cuts-only VHS system. We used the time code burn-in tapes, and if we wanted to make a new cut we had to make a new generation. So by the time we had our off-line you could hardly see it. It was really awful, and when we did the online we had to use that as our base, and sometimes it was very hard because we could hardly read the time code because it had gone through four or five different generations. Obviously, for that kind editing, those systems (Media 100s) are so revolutionary.

Chris Blasingame

We transferred to video and I was waiting for money for post. You transfer it to video and you have time code, key code, edge number, and sound time code burned in. I didn't print any film yet. I would print it if I had money because it's great to see it projected before it's finalized. We didn't have the luxury to see dailies every night.

But the process is this—we transfer, and it's a rough transfer; the colors won't exactly match from scene to scene, but we do the best we can. We get all that stuff burned in—the key code; the edge number, which is on the film; and the sound time code number—everything that locks it together in sync.

You take them on Beta tapes and you digitize them into video so the sound and picture are locked, but there are codes that refer to each frame of picture and each frame of sound. On Avid Film Composer with the film option that gives you the edit decision list, put all those numbers in so every time you make a cut, it lists all those numbers. You get a file which has all the numbers in it, and you put all that in the computer, and it's like a skeleton, and you digitize and it matches the picture or media to the skeleton.

So now you have the skeleton and you have everything in sync and you start chopping it up. When you're done chopping it up you should now be able to tell the computer to make a list, an edit decision list, so it will tell the conformer how to cut the film, and it will tell the sound guy to the frame what sound to insert here and what sound to insert there. So then you have it on paper—you have all your fades and dissolves and stuff.

Elizabeth Ledo as Lizard and George Wilson as Roadrunner take direction for their next shot.
Photo by Tim Sabo.

Now comes the really expensive part: the printing process. For video, we take that edited stuff, go online, and either retransfer or take the tapes and screw with the color. I think it's a retransfer; I'm not sure. We do an online master, which means we color-correct the scenes so it looks continuous. At the same time the sound guy is putting all original dialogue onto the sound track—he doesn't take it off the Beta tapes, he takes it off the DAT tapes, and he's putting in all fresh dialogue. And we're also putting in sound effects and music, and he's making the sound mix as we're conforming the picture.

Then we blow up the super-16mm negative to a 35mm positive master. But we can't print from a positive to a positive so we have to make an internegative so it's a single strand—and this is all like $1.45 a foot for three thousand feet, so just the internegative cost will be about $7,000. So then we take that and we conform the negative to A/B, and we print A/B to a master positive, and then it's a single strand. Then we print it to a negative dupe. So then we have our negative in 35mm and we also have the sound track. We make it dirty black and white—it's called the dirty dupe—we make a black-and-white print of the movie to sync it up. We play it to make sure it's right. We check for sync and then we start the printing. We make an answer print where we check all the timing numbers. And then we make correction prints, and at a certain point the correction prints can be used as release prints. Then we print release prints, and oh don't forget about titles. We have to do titles, and I'm sure there are a few things I'm not talking about.

We're not even done with picture yet. I need to go pick up a speedometer going one hundred miles an hour. It's fun now because I'm not worried about picture too much—now I'm thinking about sound. I had never done that to this point—I knew what we had to do for sound, but I wasn't ready to do that process. But now it's pretty close.

I will probably write the music. We synced up some stuff to it just for a reference of how I want it—trying to communicate to people. But I'm probably going to have to write it just to save money. You can convince people to have a heart and give you festival rights, telling them, "We have our film synced to your music and we invested it in our sound track. If you will give us this for free for festivals, and if it ever gets distributed, we will buy those rights from you. Then you'll make a killing off of us." That's what festival rights do. It's a gamble for them. They say, "Well we'll give them to you for free, but if you ever make money you're going to have to pay us what we want." I could do it that way but I don't really know if it's worth it. Then there's foreign distribution and all this clearance-house crap. Clearance houses don't really want to work with you unless you have a distribution deal somewhere, so it's the chicken and the egg thing. I could do the work, but I figure what the hell, I might just pay for a day and get some musicians in the studio and write some songs.

I wish everybody in the process could sit in on the editing session. It was Elizabeth Ledo's first movie and she did a great job, but as an actress she would benefit from sitting in on an editing session. Because nobody really ever thinks about matching shots and matching dynamics and matching flow, and if you're a director and you've never sat in on an editing session you're a fool. It's a learning process seeing all this stuff come together in editing, learning the tricks, and seeing what you can get away with. Editing is so key.

Chad Etchison

I think the very beginning sets up what has to happen, and there are enough elements of danger. The first three minutes set up the occult underpinnings. And then we have a major shift and we're suddenly in the bright outside, and the two characters are talking about this character they're going to have to kill, Harlan McCoy. Then we shift to the sheriff's deputy and there's a comedic thing happening. Then we meet Harlan finally. So that first ten minutes sets up what's going to happen to Harlan. That definitely was on my mind—I didn't want it to open and be nothingness—there had to be something to grab them and be weird. I wanted them to wonder, "What in the world is going on here?" That's important. The film is like a song—you want your song to start off and have something to interest the audience so that they have a reason to sit there for the next two hours.

I think my film has a slow build-up. I was trying to do a Roman Polanski *Chinatown* thing where you're gathering clues and hopefully you have enough interest in the protagonist that you care about the clues. You're kind of peeking—you know the end result and you know who did it and you know why, and now you're interested in watching Jack find out. That's the mystery. How's he going to find out—how is the story going to unravel? You already know who did it. You know the end result. That's not the question—it's, "How is it going to be resolved?" So hopefully he's an interesting enough character that you'll end up wanting to see him solve this thing and come out of it. And hopefully he'll be likable. That's the main thing—I hope that's what I did—if I didn't do that I failed because I don't want him to be an unlikable character where nobody really cares what happens. I don't want people to think, "Who cares? It's boring because we don't like any of these people." Even though they're doing bad things, hopefully they're likable. They're based on people I know.

It took ten days to sync it and we've been creative editing for about

(From left) Mack Murrah is Jack Collins and Chad Etchison is Mike Best, in *The Initiate*. © 2000 Etch-Me Films. Photo by P. Daniel Maughon.

two and a half weeks. We are about twenty minutes into the film with the edit. We're going to have a rough cut six weeks from now. It'll take two months to get the rough cut and then take another month fine-tuning that. Then we'll do sound and music—that'll probably take another three months realistically—that would be great but I don't know.

I think the film looks exactly the way we planned it. There are so many cuts per scene there's never a dull moment. Camera-wise, it is incredible—I am blown away by it. The performances are great. It all goes back to the script—if the script was any good, if the story was interesting at all, and if it was shot well and acted well, then it could be a great film. And it was shot well—no doubt about that. And I think acted well. But if the story was mediocre then it'll be a mediocre film. It's hard for me to say, but I think that people find the story interesting. It's a typical story, but I took a very typical type of scenario and tried to shoot it in such a way to make it interesting. I think that's what every film is. Some stories are magnificent and really original. This is not what I would call an original storyline, but what's interesting about it is the way it's shot. We took

117

an old formula and approached it from our angle and hopefully the way we came at it will be interesting for people to watch. I feel really positive about it right now. But it's so hard for me to judge.

Directing is the thing I think you would learn from a short. If you directed and shot and edited a short, and then went to make a feature, you wouldn't make the same mistakes. There were several times in the beginning of the film that I would forget to make the actors step into frame or wipe the frame, and even if you're never going to use that in editing, you need to do it. You'll recognize that in editing because the couple of times I forgot, I thought, "Man, there he is stuck flat on his mark and we needed him to step into his mark." So there are little things like that that as a first-time person you don't know. There were a lot of things we were doing as we were filming and I would think, "Why are we doing this? What is this thing for? What's this thing gonna do?" And now I know.

We don't have to reshoot anything. We still have some second-unit stuff to shoot and there's one small MOS (*mit* out sound) dream sequence that remains to be shot that we may or may not live without, but I think we'll end up shooting it. But as far as reshooting material, we don't have to do that.

I'm working on getting a score composed. I have a musical background—some of the rock music was some of the music I had written—but I really wanted a Bernard Herman, Alex North type of a score like the Hitchcock sound. I really wanted to get that sound across because I think that may be an interesting new take for younger filmmakers—to make something that has something from older films but different from the rock-and-roll energy or the seventies thing. I wanted to do something new and different. I love watching Hitchcock over any other filmmaker, except maybe Lynch, and their music includes these compositions, so why don't I go the extra mile and get that done?

We're actually looking into having the Atlanta Symphony Orchestra record a real symphony. It's going to cost a ton I'm sure, but, if anything, I think music and sound can elevate this film. Your story is only as good

Director Chad Etchison confers with actor Mack Murrah during filming of *The Initiate*. © 2000 Etch-Me Films. Photo by P. Daniel Maughon.

as it is, but I think there are things you can do to hopefully get people to love the film and say, "You know, that movie has been done before, and I've seen that story, but there was something about the music in that film." Or, "I like the way that film looked—it had a feel to it." If that's something that happens, I'll be very excited. I know certain films that I don't think are perfect—and they're by great directors, especially some of Lynch's stuff, especially some of the films he's done recently, the films between *Blue Velvet* and *Lost Highway*—but they had something about them. He takes chances and it's interesting. It's more interesting to me than watching a movie that's like you've seen a billion times. If it provokes some sort of emotional response that's the main thing that I want to see happen.

After Chad had been in post for a year, he reported: We are on the second pass of editing; we have one cut that is completed but much too long. After the third pass we should have it. So far we have been cutting a year, it's a long process, but it has to be done correctly and we can't start tak-

119

ing short cuts at this stage in the film's development. I feel very confident that we have made a good film, at least by my standards. It looks beautiful and I think the characterizations and story are strong.

After Chad had been in post for over eighteen months, he reported: I am currently in the final stages of postproduction on *The Initiate* at Todd-AO Studios in Atlanta, Georgia. Final mixing is scheduled for completion on January 15, 2000. Release prints will be struck and the film will be available for distribution to the international festival circuit in winter of 2000.

7

Festivals/Distribution— While You Were Screening

The maze to finding success with festivals and distribution is a megillah unto itself. Some turns take a political bent; other paths are more independent or progressive in character.

Once your course carries you into the media maelstrom you will confront publicity from admirers and nonadmirers, praise from nameworthy and noteworthy, rejection from same, contact with potential benefactors or mentors, and the genesis of a reputation, your own. You might even garner the elusive green.

But the long and short of it is you are launched on your journey, and it is all critical to your evolution as a filmmaker.

Michael Shoob

Michael Shoob and his producing partner Daniel Linck practiced a bit of stealth research to get their feet in the distribution doors. They began going to film markets and seminars to make industry contacts. But they also snuck into numerous parties at Sundance to gain exposure and shake the hands of people who would be able to help them with advertising and screenings down the road. And their strategy worked well. *Driven* was first screened at the Floating Film Festival. Then it was on to Toronto, the Hamptons, and Slamdance, where it won Honorable Mention and attracted the attention of their now foreign-sales company.

Driven garnered screen time at the following international festivals and venues:

- Floating Film Festival
- Paramount (industry screening for an audience of one thousand)
- First Look (independent showcase at the Tribeca Film Center, New York)
- Toronto Film Festival
- Hamptons Film Festival (New York)
- Palm Springs Film Festival
- Slamdance (Honorable Mention for the best film of the 1997 festival)
- South by Southwest Film Festival (Austin, Texas)
- Taos Talking Picture Festival (Taos, New Mexico)
- High Museum (Atlanta, Georgia)
- The University of Southern California
- The University of California (Irvine, California)
- The University of California (Riverside, California)
- Broadcast: April 22, 1998 on KCET, Los Angeles at 9 P.M.
- Theatrical Opening: April 24, 1998, Laemmle Monica Fourplex SoCal's Cinemapolis

I am a little wary about trusting the evaluations of a single audience. Films play differently every night. At Toronto, at the Hamptons, at Paramount, in one screening the movie can play adequately. In another, perhaps fueled by a number of audience members who connect very powerfully and spread their enthusiasm through the theater, the feeling can be quite electric. One audience laughs from beginning to end. Another sits in their seats and never laughs, but also never moves—they are riveted. Still, both audiences seem to love the film.

By the way, showing the film almost always makes me crazy. I pace the back of the theater. I pummel whatever producer, editor, DP, or friend within striking distance. I take a long walk and hope something good happens. And I come back and usually enjoy watching the credits roll.

At Toronto, films show a number of times. Unfortunately, many festivals now have a policy of having press-industry screenings, which segregate the critics from general audiences. My personal feeling is that this is not a very good idea. Audiences can surprise critics, and ultimately affect their evaluation of a picture.

For example, Frank Scheck of the *Hollywood Reporter* reviewed the film. He was in the press-industry screening at the Hamptons. He had very nice things to say about me and ultimately about the picture as well. But he didn't think audiences would understand the picture. It was "too weird." Now, had he been in one of our public screenings at the Hamptons or at Toronto or even with Chantal Westerman of *Good Morning America* at a screening she hosted in Irvine, he would have seen and heard audiences from ages twenty-five to seventy evaluating the picture. Certainly, the movie touched many of them, but because Mr. Scheck didn't see it, well, he wouldn't know it. The film is a little unconventional, but hardly inaccessible.

At any rate, the audiences in Toronto were quite rewarding. They love films. They ask good questions afterwards, and they filled both of our public screenings. The Hamptons was also a good crowd. The venue, unfortunately, wasn't as good. Theaters were smaller and not as good technically.

Actually, one of the most rewarding elements for me has been to be able to discuss the film with audiences afterwards. My ambition with *Driven* was to give folks something provocative, something to chew on. It's a terrific thrill to respond to questions, to watch an audience work a little to come to grips with the film. It's a full-bodied response, better than "we loved it." After all, it took a lot of agonizing to make. It's nice to see audiences have to do a little thinking as well. It's only fair.

123

At Toronto, I did a number of print and television interviews for the film. Judy Gerstel, critic for the *Toronto Star,* suggested that she do her interview with me in a cab as we drove around the city.

I liked the idea and so we climbed into a cab that we flagged down at random. The driver was a young Pakistani. He proceeded to echo just about everything I had told her and virtually everything we had shown in the film: the danger of the job, the frenetic search for fares, and his own dream of success. He had tried one business venture and failed; he was saving to try another.

I think that the chemistry between this Toronto driver and me was such that Gerstel's piece ended up on the front page, right in the middle of the festival. It helped me to fill our screening that day.

I've occasionally found that critics, unfamiliar with the world of cab driving, simply question whether I've drawn the world accurately. One critic actually wrote, "What is most unbelievable about the film is the high level of anger and stress . . . the men behave as if being a taxi driver required the same feverish intensity as working on the floor of the New York Stock Exchange." Well, guess what? It often does. I think this critic, though he said quite nice things about the work, displayed the worse kind of white-collar bias. Somehow, many folks in America think that blue-collar jobs don't require the fire that more high-profile occupations require. They couldn't be more wrong. One of my producers said to me, "I was more intense as a waiter fighting for tables than I am as a producer." And one recent newspaper article cited cab driving as the fourth most stressful job in the world next to brain surgery and the presidency.

It's ironic. One of the reasons I wanted to make this film was to have audiences live in the cab-driving world. I wouldn't have dreamed that a few folks wouldn't believe it was true. I half expected that some might just not be interested, but I never thought credibility would be an issue.

We have not made a video deal for the picture yet, and we've had a curious anomaly involving the picture in cable. Because we did a token southern California release of the film kicked off by a sneak preview in prime time on KCET (PBS), Showtime (although they wanted the film)

Jennifer Wynne Farmer and her "kids," (left to right) Tiffany Ellen Solano, Sy Hearn, Christopher Ogden, and Shawn Pyfrom, with her son Austin on her lap. © Pumpkin Pictures LLC.

felt that they couldn't acquire the picture because of this one small TV airing—at least right now. Negotiations are continuing.

In the last month, a newly formed company has asked to acquire the domestic rights, and we're in discussions with them.

Jennifer Farmer

I was not sure that *Pumpkin Man* would ever have a festival shelf life because it is a precious, warm, darling half-hour family film. I'm finding that there are a handful of film festivals that celebrate that and encourage that. The Santa Clarita International Film Festival is the only film festival in the world fully dedicated to family-oriented films and programming. So there's a home for my films and me in the future. *Pumpkin Man* was a finalist in the 1998 Santa Clarita International Film Festival and in Worldfest Houston. It also won the Dove Seal and the Film Advisory Board award for excellence in family programming.

Sundance came to us while we were making *Naturally Native* and

125

amazingly enough asked if we would world premiere at the 1998 Sundance Film Festival, which is something that just never happens. We were amazed and excited and worked twenty-four hours a day seven days a week to get it finished in time to do that. We took it up there and they realized it was an important film and something worthy of being shown there, and it was met with huge success by distributors, press, media, and viewers. We were very excited about that. Then we had distributor screenings because that really kind of launched the film and put us all on the map a bit.

The USA Film Festival in Dallas, Texas, in mid-April also has a family film section. We sent both films to the New York Women's Film Festival in April 1998 for display. Seeing as how both movies were produced, written, directed, key departmented, and edited by women, we thought that would be of particular interest.

So there are all kinds of film festivals; you just have to find your niche. Look on the Internet under film festivals and you'll find the list of hundreds worldwide and find the ones that are really good. Because *Pumpkin Man* was going directly to television and/or directly to video, we do not have a film print. So there are a lot of film festivals we cannot enter because they will only accept a final film version of the film.

Naturally Native ended up winning four to five prestigious awards at film festivals such as Dreamspeakers Festival in Alberta, Canada and Worldfest Flagstaff International Film Festival. Both films have pending distribution deals for television, video, and theatrical release in the fall of 1999.

Ali Selim

We had a great premiere in St. Paul in the neighborhood where we shot. Over one thousand people came and seemed to love it. We thought it was a winner.

Then the festival rejections stormed in. Nearly one a day for a month and a half. I could hardly get out of bed in the morning. The mail carrier coming down the block looked to me to be the Grim Reaper. Later

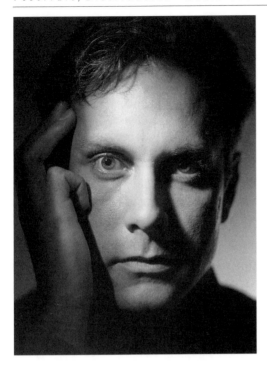

Ali Selim, director of *Emperor of the Air*. Photo by John Lehn.

in the summer I received some nice letters from festival directors explaining that the reasons for the rejections were largely the film's length (not a short, not a feature) and the film's verbosity (it wouldn't play well to a non-English speaking audience).

Emperor was screened at the Minneapolis International Film Festival, the Vienna Film Critics Circle Festival where it won Best in Show, Houston WorldFest where it won the Gold Award, WorldFest Charleston where it won the Silver Award, the Metropolitan Film Festival of Atlanta, and the Cucaloris Film Festival in North Carolina. The film has won first and second places at a handful of festivals, and in going to them and watching other films I learned that film festivals are really about commerce for the city. They are like conventions that fill hotel rooms and restaurants, and they are programmed as such. What is fun? What will draw in people? What will get them back out to the restaurants in two hours?

If I had it to do all over again, I would make exactly the same film. I

127

made exactly the film I wanted to make. If I were given the assignment to win festivals I would make a film under ten minutes and make it nothing but funny.

Traci Carroll

Our film premiered at the Atlanta Film and Video Festival in June of 1998. I think the Atlanta festival is the oldest and largest of the festivals that we've been in with maybe the exception of Raindance Film Showcase—they're not as old but they may be as big. The guy that projected my film in the Atlanta festival has his own festival in Baltimore; he ordered the film for that festival and we got two screenings up there. His film festival is an underground festival, and our film in a lot of ways is not a great fit with his festival because the kind of stuff that he generally does is low budget and ours is definitely not low budget. It was what he called substream, which is a phrase he is trying to coin because independent is not really independent anymore. I think our film is a good match with that sort of ideology. So we went there and we got into Raindance, which was great, and they were really supportive of our film. I felt that because it was a juried festival and they take so few shorts in comparison with the number of entries they get, it was good for our film.

We went to the Freaky Film Festival in Illinois. The reason I entered that one was because there's a guy who had a couple of short films in Atlanta and I really liked his style, and I saw that his films had been on the previous year's program. And I thought, "Oh cool. If they like his film then they might like my film, too." And we got a great review from them, a great response from the Ohio festival, and we're going to California and to Florida.

Particularly and ironically, the women's festivals have not liked the film. A festival got my name—it's a very small festival—and sent me a brochure and a letter saying, "Please send a tape. We screen all our stuff and we're just trying to promote women filmmakers." So I sent it and they sent it back with a letter that said although your film is very visually appealing and very high quality we feel like it plays on the exact

Lauri Faggioni as Veronica in *Five O'clock Shadow*.

stereotype we are trying to dispel with our festival. And I thought that was so ironic because the Freaky Festival in Illinois was sponsored by the Women's Studies at Illinois. There's two diametrically opposed points of view on my film. So I wrote this woman a letter and said, "I think you've missed the point of my film." And I outlined that it is a very subjective film and that you can interpret it any way you want to. One woman who saw the film in the Atlanta festival came up to me afterward and said, "I wanted to tell you that I loved everything about it except the script." And then she started in on me, "As a feminist I don't know how you could make a film that shows women in this light." But it's her perception that they're shown in that light because you can then flip it around and see it the other way, too. (The film is intentionally left open to interpretation.)

We had two screenings at the Palm Beach International Film Festival. They were really enthusiastic about our film and about me coming down with it, and they actually volunteered to pay for a hotel. It's weird how some festivals are into it and some festivals aren't. We got rejected from everything in Park City, Utah, the Sundance, Slamdance, No Dance, all the Park City festivals, and South by Southwest. I think that those festivals aren't really for independent films, and it's all about who's attached to your film. That's why there's Slamdance, but Slamdance has rapidly become that way because there are so many films that aren't getting into Sundance because there's not enough room. So Park City is really driven by the politics and there's not a lot of truly independent stuff being shown there.

Then there are other festivals like the Cleveland festival that are older established festivals and have a certain audience that expects certain types of films. Their patrons come to see the same thing every year and if you have anything too weird or outlandish they're going to feel like the festival is not something they want to support anymore. Festivals really worry about maintaining their audiences. Even Atlanta is a little like that—the Atlanta festival has been around for twenty years and they try to support the local filmmakers, but they're also trying to hold onto and expand the audience. A lot of the time it means expanding it to the middle-class suburban type people who are used to seeing their mainstream Hollywood films in the theater, and they don't know what to do with really *avant-garde* or independent substream type films.

Subsequent festival activity has included the Fringe Fest and the Paradigm Shift in Atlanta, Georgia, the Utah Short Film and Video Festival, the Euro Underground Festival in Krakow, Poland, the St. Louis International Film Festival, and the St. Louis New Year's Eve Event. The film also received an Honorable Mention from the Rochester International Film Fest.

The festivals I personally am most interested in are the festivals that are under ten years old, that are trying to make a name for themselves by showing stuff that you don't see every day. And those are the festivals that we have gotten the most support from, and those are the festivals that are most enthusiastic about our film. I've been really happy with the response we've gotten, and I guess I knew going into it that we did a very abstract, very subjective film; I knew it wasn't going to be the best film at Sundance. I've never felt like we've been slighted. It's important to enter the festivals because you never know who's going to see your film, but at the same time I don't hold my breath for the larger festivals because I know that our film is not a good fit for those types of festivals. It's really the more underground, substream, off-independent, or whatever you want to call it—those types of festivals are really the ones most interested in a type of film like ours.

As far as festivals, I think of them as a résumé. You can say, "I've been in these festivals," and what people see from that is, "This person has been in festivals." And it's great if you're in Sundance or South by Southwest because you can pretty much write your own ticket if you have a feature-length film that shows in one of those. If you have a short film it doesn't matter in a lot of ways where it shows—it just matters that it shows. I think it also shows people, when you're trying to get them to back you when you're doing a feature, that you have the follow-through to go all the way through the process, that you're behind your film from beginning to end.

Also important is the chance to meet people at festivals. To me it's not so much about getting the film in the festivals as it is about going and hooking up with somebody. Jim and I went to Sundance and happened to be at this restaurant sitting at the bar. This guy who had come in at the same time as us was sitting next to me, obviously alone, poor guy. So I said, "Hey are you a filmmaker, too?" And he said, "No, I'm a producer at Paramount." So we had this great conversation. He was the nicest person and was totally in love with the South and wants to come here and visit. You never know who you might meet. It's all about meeting people and having a good connection. Filmmakers are a great connection because you have that in common and you never know who they know.

I am now winding down on the festivals. The film has been on the festival circuit for over eighteen months, which is great since short films don't have much of a life after the festivals. I have talked to several distributors about possibilities for the film's distribution.

I have also talked to a lot of Internet distributors that would like to stream our film over the Internet, but I have been warned by several people, from both the production and distribution end, that putting our film on the Internet will greatly limit our chances for broadcast distribution. (Although we do sell copies of it from our Web site.) It makes sense, so I'm still waiting to see if someone will pick it up.

David Zeiger

Displaced in the New South went to a lot of festivals. First, we took *Displaced* to the Independent Feature Film Market (IFFM) as a work in progress. We did a fourteen-minute piece for them, and we got great response to it there. We got contacted by some television people and by some educational distributors, and then when it was finished we just started submitting to festivals.

We received money from the Corporation for Public Broadcasting for editing. It was a regional designation contract. There are these regional organizations around here called the Southern Educational Communications Association (SECA), and if you're coproducing with a PBS station you can submit proposals. It's basically for money to go to projects that either are being produced by the PBS stations or are coproductions with independents. We got $10,000 through that—it's a contract, not a grant. Basically, it was a PBS purchase of the film for broadcast. It went out on what's called the soft feed, which means it's fed to the PBS stations by SECA, not by the national PBS headquarters. All the stations got it and basically looked at it and decided whether or not to air it. And it got pretty good airplay. We got scattered reports, but we never got a full accounting of what stations it was on.

Through the festivals we got the attention of educational distributors. There's a festival called the National Educational Media Competition every year—it's a big deal. They hand out awards: the Bronze Apple, Silver Apple, and Gold Apple. We got the Bronze Apple. Every big educational distributor in the country immediately inundated us. They basically go after everything that gets an award at this thing. We had a fun time actually being able to choose—it was the first time with that

(From left) David Zeiger's son, Danny, Mary Ellen Wiggins, and Brett keep warm during a game. © 1998 Displaced LLC. Photo by Mike Kandrach.

film that we were in the driver's seat. We weren't competing with a bunch of other films to get a grant—there were all these distributors competing with each other to get us.

We ended up with the University of California Extension Center for Media and Independent Learning who has done a great job of distributing. Through them and through festivals we got the attention of some international television. Actually it was through a thing called the SVSTV in Australia—a public TV network in Australia. They bought it. The biggest thing that happened was Discovery Channel International. They have an international network that goes to about two hundred countries. They had seen it at the festival, and they were putting together a series on immigration and they bought it for that. That was actually our biggest sale.

There's a lot of money in the educational market. Festivals, I think, are one of the main ways to get seen by distributors and by television networks and by those kinds of folks. There are all the organizations—the National Organization for Independent Film, the Organizations for

International Documentary Association, AIVF (Association of Independent Video and Filmmakers)—that are always publishing calendars for festivals and competitions. They put out books about the various grants available and those kinds of things. Those publications and organizations are really good to follow and to join.

We are trying to get *The Band* into festivals. The *POV* thing is the biggest thing—that's our TV broadcast. I have a guy who distributes documentaries to international television. I met him when we were doing *Displaced* and he became our distributor for that, so he's acting as our distributor for *The Band*. There's all these international marketplaces for television programming where all programmers go when they're buying products, and he's taking it all around to those.

So we're submitting it to festivals and getting turned down left and right, and it's really bizarre. I still haven't gotten a complete handle on what problems people are having with it. One thing that is good about the IFFM is that there are a lot of people who are big names in independent films—people who act as advisors and producers' reps. Some of them have become very well known. There's John Pierson, who has this show on the Independent Film Channel, and he goes to the IFFM. And then there's this guy named Bob Hawk who is considered a big name who can make things happen. He loved *The Band* at the IFFM and called me up and said it was the best film there—this is when it was there as a work in progress. Since then he has actually been my advisor on it and he has given me a lot of helpful feedback on cuts, and he has also been recommending it to festivals. It is high on his list of recommendations to festivals, but even with that it's not getting in. He says that there's a lot of good competition out there right now—this just happens to be a very good year for festivals. I agree and disagree because I've gotten to know a lot of films that are big in the festivals. Some of them are great. But in my opinion, and of course it's subjective, some of them can't hold a candle to *The Band*. And what can you say? I'm obviously not the most objective person on the planet about this.

It's an extremely subjective business—there's just no getting around it—some things hit big because of things other than their quality. To me the prime example this year is *The Big One* by Michael Moore.

I talked to the head of acquisitions for Miramax because he actually called me. He loved *The Band*. He had seen it at the IFFM and really enjoyed it, and I had sent the finished product to him—this is the kind of thing that can happen—and he called me and said he really liked it. He wasn't sure that it would do well as a theatrical film but he was open to that possibility and he wasn't going to make any decisions about it until he saw it at festivals to see what kind of audience response it got. So we submitted to Sundance, and Bob Hawk is an advisor to Sundance, and we were on his list. And then of course it didn't get in. The reality is that if you don't get into Sundance you end up with a huge strike against you with a lot of things—with other festivals. But also this guy didn't get a chance to see it with an audience. Then *POV* picked us up. And the *POV* broadcast ended the possibility of it being a theatrical broadcast because you've essentially wiped out your theatrical audience by being on TV. We would have been idiots to turn down *POV* in the hopes that Miramax was going to bite.

Chris Blasingame

The outcome after editing is expected and unexpected. I'm happy with it. I never thought going into it that it would be a masterpiece. I never thought it would be the only film I got to shoot. I liked the story because I wrote it and put so much behind it. But I looked at what I was competing against and what I didn't like about what I was competing against, and I also looked at the budget competition, like people trying to make features for $50,000 or people trying to do the impossible for that kind of money. I just decided that I'm going to try to do something that's going to stick out. Like I said, I don't think it's my masterpiece by any means, but I do think it sticks out.

I don't want to make a personal artsy emotional piece of crap that nobody would understand and wouldn't get me anywhere. So I tried to make a story that's accessible to a lot of people and also to make it very

Elizabeth Ledo takes direction in *Roadrunner*. Photo by Tim Sabo.

bizarre. Roadrunner's rantings are a high point for me—they're interesting to me and they satisfied my appetite to be very creative and off the wall, but the story is very accessible to everybody. Nobody will think, "Oh that's deep," or "That's a very personal film." So I think it succeeded in those ways, and I'm happy with that.

The next step is to really start going to festivals and getting attention. Look at me, look at me, look at me, give me money—that kind of thing. I will apply to everything. I've never done this before. I will look through the festivals and find which ones it might apply to. There are a lot that it automatically won't be appropriate for, and there are a lot of festivals that are more family oriented that profanity won't be appropriate in, but there are a lot of other ones that I think it will be great in.

I think we want to earn a reputation, and obviously what we want to do as a company is make features that will make money for our investors. We don't really want to spend more money on shorts that aren't going to go anywhere. But we recognize the fact that we didn't have the money to make a feature the way we wanted to, so the money was best spent on a short. We might win some prizes but we're not expecting to break the bank off this short.

So the next thing we will do is make a feature for a good amount of money, but not a lot of money. We won't tell anybody how much we spent; we won't discuss the production with anybody; we'll get the entire thing in the can so nobody can want changes, and we'll print it. People will have more pressure to take it as is. We'll get it into festivals and get it seen as a feature and try to get a distribution deal. I would have gone on and shot a feature if I had the money, but I didn't think the money was best spent on a watered-down feature. I couldn't have shot *Cold Ground* for $50,000 in any way—I don't care who says they could have. It wouldn't have been good. So I want to get investors. I want to get the reputation and get investors, and I want to be open to a lot more investors by getting exposure, and I want to put together the money for *Cold Ground*. So that's what it's all for.

Chad Etchison

I want to finish it and try to go through this whole festival circuit, which I don't know anything about. When I was in the music business we went through all the showcases, so I'm assuming it's similar. It's probably political and completely frustrating, so I'm already preparing myself for the worst. I'm definitely prepared to be miserable. It's gonna suck and it'll probably be really disappointing—you spend all this time and then somebody can see it and say that it's not the direction they want to take, and then it's over. And that means you didn't make your money back, or maybe you'll sell it in an international video market. And nobody gives one single anything and your name didn't go anywhere, and it's like, "Well I made a film but who cares?" That's the reality. Hopefully I'll be one of the lucky ones and I'll win the lottery and my name will come out above the other people's. I don't know if it will or not.

I'm definitely going to make another film. I think that if I give up after one film it would be hasty. If I give up after two, it probably would be a good idea. If I give up after one, though, I think I would have to shoot myself in the foot. I think I should try again because I think by the way this film looks I will get interest to do another one hopefully. Who knows? You'd be surprised by how little people really care—you think you're doing something great, but nobody cares. It's weird. It's really bizarre.

We are hoping to enter Sundance as well as every other major festival. The festival route seems very much a politically paved road; who knows what will happen! A plan is helpful though. We have talked to a couple of press agents as well as reps that can help us with that process. I'm somewhat dreading that part of things.

8

Producing/Directing— Citizen Sane?

irecting and producing an independent film is giving birth. While
in the throes of labor you swear you will never dance this tango
again. But once you've delivered your love child, all the pain seems to
fade into distant memory and you are again ready to burn up the dance
floor. Advice from veterans of the dance: wear thick-soled shoes.

As the conductor of your concerto, you embrace stamina, faith, and
humor. You must, of course, rehearse for your journey, but stay loose
enough to allow for impromptu passages along the way. You must retain
the vision of your opus when dealing with the minutia of each movement. You must also gamble and jump blindly when bridges aren't
apparent. And, as maestro, you must lead by example and possess the
people skills to maintain positive morale if your set turns sour.

The toll is high, but so is the reward. You did it, and you did it your
way.

Michael Shoob

I would probably drop any of them (writing, producing, or directing) if
the right opportunity comes along. I would be delighted to direct (with-

Director Michael Shoob confers with Director of Photography Joseph Mealey, on the set of *Driven*.

out writing the script). I would be delighted to direct and merely rewrite somebody else so I would have a touch of detachment from the writing process, which would be fun. I would be more than happy to have a wonderful, terrific person take on all the producing responsibilities that take a great deal of time away from the creative work. On the other hand, I'm more than willing to do all three again—if it gives me a chance to make a film my own way.

Since *Driven,* I have been working on writing a new movie to direct, in meetings about directing a movie for a German company (from someone else's script), and in talks about various TV projects. There has even been some interest in *Driven* as a kind of ensemble TV series. In November of 1999, it premiered on Pay Per View on Direct TV around the country with additional play on cable, and hopefully its debut on video will come through during the year 2000.

Most recently, I am preparing to direct *First Comes Love* from a screenplay by Alan Hines (*Square Dance*) based on the critically acclaimed memoir by Marion Winik.

Jennifer Wynne Farmer (right) talking with 2nd AD Laura Johnson, on the set of *Pumpkin Man*. © Pumpkin Pictures LLC.

Jennifer Farmer

While there were similar job duties and experiences on both films, there were a lot of differences as well. On *Pumpkin Man* I was executive producer, producer, and director. On *Naturally Native* I simply operated in the codirector capacity, and I did a lot of coproducing on the side for Valerie Red Horse who was the executive producer, writer, lead actress, and just about everything else.

As a producer and a director I was under incredible pressure. I carried the burden of responsibility for everything, and of course there is a lot of pressure. But there is a way to have pressure and to have an awful lot of fun. It was probably one of the most pleasurable things I have ever done. It's a rush and a high—and I don't ride roller coasters or fast rides at the amusement parks—but I can't imagine anything being more exciting or more fun or more pleasurable. Even when things got tough.

141

You have the weight of the world on your shoulders. It's up to you to make it work. On your say-so, things will go well or not go well. That's a whole lot of pressure. And every dollar you need to account for, and that needs to matter. I've always said that in the end credits of a film there is no place for excuses—there is no place to say we didn't have enough time; we didn't have enough money; I had to use so and so's daughter in the part and I didn't want to; I didn't have time to reshoot. There is no place for excuses. So when the movie is all said and done you need to stand by it and say, "This is the film—like it or not here it is." We're in a very no-excuses industry—no-excuses business. You need to take the praise or the blame, and only the receiving audience can tell you which one you'll be receiving.

We coped with it with a lot of prayer. On *Naturally Native* we began every day with a prayer. For those who were available and interested in wanting to participate, we had a meeting place where every morning we would have prayer and gather. I think that added a lot to the unity and family spirit of the film. On *Pumpkin Man* we did it on a smaller scale. I began and ended every day with prayer—prayer of thanks and prayer of openness and prayer of seeking assistance. I was divinely blessed on both films beyond my greatest expectations.

I was out there doing stand-up comedy fourteen hours a day making sure that everybody was having a good time and that the stress of filmmaking never got anybody too upset. It was great. It mattered. And when you're having that kind of fun making a film, I believe it transfers to the big screen and somehow, some way, it is noticeable and there is an energy perceived by the audience. That's exactly what happened in both films.

The biggest obstacles are actually completing the darn thing. Getting it in the can, having no casualties, getting it done, and getting it into post are the biggest obstacles. Many films are made everyday in this world that never see the light of post.

The gratification is doing it. The gratification is that you want to make a T-shirt that says, "I survived the filmmaking process." Realizing that you accomplished what you set out to do is probably the greatest gratification.

I cannot imagine ever doing anything else—it was such an exhilarating process, such a joy to do. An awful lot of hard work. I can't imagine any work being harder than it was, but it was so much fun and so rewarding that I can't imagine doing anything else. The greatest reward is to tell a good story that's character driven, that has something to say, and that makes you think. I want people to come to a Jenn Farmer film and walk away and say, "Something's happened to me—I'm a little bit better person for having seen that piece of filmmaking."

Producers are the ones that have the final say and the ultimate creative control. If you're going to go to the trouble of making a film you might as well have that creative control. The director—that's what I have been given the gift of doing, and that's what I need to do.

People skills are probably the number one advantage to any kind of filmmaking. Having good people skills; evoking a good performance out of the cast, out of the crew, out of the PAs, out of the studio people, a good performance out of the investors; and being able to have people share and believe in your beliefs and vision and stories is absolutely paramount to the success of any director. I hear stories about directors who are screamers and yellers and whiners and that sort of thing, and how it is that they can get up in the morning and actually believe that they can continue having a career I don't know. Filmmaking is so hard, being unkind and inhumane seems absolutely unacceptable and beyond reason to me.

Independent filmmaking is really coming into its own right now. The studios and the world are really paying attention to independent filmmaking like they never have before. With the huge success of the Sundance Film Festival and Sundance Channel and all of the nurturing outlets that independent filmmaking is finding right now, it's a very legitimate form of filmmaking. I've always said that low-budget filmmaking doesn't have to mean low class. And we are seeing that more and more in filmmaking today, so this is the most exciting time to be an independent filmmaker, certainly as an independent woman filmmaker, as there are lots of opportunities opening up that way.

You gain full creative control because you can tell whatever story you want the way you want to tell it and in the style in which you want to tell it. It is a wonderful thing. Having to raise your own funding and do it all yourself is the drawback. Having studio backing, you know where it's going to land when you're done with it. That is certainly a comfort zone, provided that the studio allows you to make the film in a like-minded way and that they aren't going to have people causing you to be a robot on the set to serve their needs and wishes. That relationship needs to be strong. There are pros and cons to both. In the future I will continue to enjoy independent filmmaking but wouldn't mind the creature comforts of studio backing.

Directing is really my great love and great passion. I want to hang onto producing for the creative control and to make sure the vision is realized, but directing is really what my future holds.

I did go to film school, and I think any education that life brings you, you can bring to filmmaking. The more you know the more able you are to spend money wisely and to not be taken by those who might realize that you are inexperienced, and there are many of those out there. As you travel across the very dangerous land mine of postproduction, the more you know and the better educated you are, the more ammunition you have for success.

I'm not going to try to be a writer or an editor or a composer or anything else. I'm going to try to continue directing. I want to find good scripts that are character driven, that are important and powerful and meaningful and have something to say, particularly in the area of family filmmaking with things for everyone to enjoy. And right now I'm going to look to a couple weeks of rest. I got up at six in the morning on February 1, 1997, and began *Pumpkin Man* and have gone one year without a day off. So I am going to come back from the premier at Foxwoods and enjoy the Santa Clarita Festival for *Pumpkin Man* for one week, and I'm going to take a couple weeks off and rest.

So I want to do it all, and I want to do it well, and I want to do it frequently.

As for updates regarding current projects, we currently have four projects in development here at Pumpkin Pictures, and one additional one in preproduction that is scheduled to shoot in February 2000. It is a movie of the week entitled, *They May Be Angels*. It is a beautiful story about the recovery of several accident and stroke victims through the use of animal-assisted therapy and is based on actual events. With this project, along with the others in development, we look forward to continuing our successful track record of telling rich, human stories to inspire and comfort our viewers.

Ali Selim

Emperor of the Air was noticed by agents in Hollywood, and I signed with one who is now trying to get me television work, which I think would be interesting but is certainly not a long-term goal for me. The film spent two good years on the festival circuit, winning some, losing others. I also have a short film distributor who is having minor success—most of it coming from Europe. An educational film distributor who has been a champion for me is carrying it, but I think it is too long for that market.

I also have two feature scripts and a television pilot that I have written and would like to produce, but I have decided that I would only like to do them on my own terms. I have made enough commercials with someone looking over my shoulder to know that I don't want someone looking over my shoulder while I make something I truly care about. I guess I would rather they weren't made than made painfully. It may happen, it may not.

I will never make a short again, so the next round of financing will be big and long. I have finished a script called *So Many Dreams*. It is a feature length love story between a Norwegian immigrant farmer and his mail-order German bride that takes place on a wheat farm in northern Minnesota during World War I. It is actually sort of a comedy; people laugh at all the right places, at least. The script (and its writer) were

145

Peter Syversten, from *Emperor of the Air*. Photo by Mike Welckle.

invited to participate in the first Cygnus Emerging Filmmakers Institute Workshop. They staged a reading in L.A. in October 1999, and I am now working on a rewrite and casting with a couple of mentors. The film is targeted to be produced in September 2000 with me directing and Gil Bellows producing.

My true love is telling stories, and I can do that with an audience of one and make a living doing something else. Making movies is fun, but you know what they say, "Pound for pound, your art dollar is better spent on sculpture than on film."

Traci Carroll

Brian Turner and I both produced the film in that we wrote it and edited it and sat down and figured out the shots together and the whole filmmaking process. But as far as producing, when it came to coordinating the crew, keeping track of all the financial and administrative stuff like festival entries, keeping track of the vendors, making sure we

First AC, David McLean, and Director, Traci Carroll, set up a shot.

got prints of our film—90 percent of that stuff I've done by myself. We started out divvying stuff up, but stuff wasn't getting done, and I was the only one doing it. Then the more I did the more I did. Administrative, organizational stuff—I realized I have a natural aptitude for that and that's why I continued to take it on. I felt I understood what needed to be done, and I felt like I was the kind of person who could motivate people to do what I wanted, or to get them to give me what I needed in order to keep things moving. And even now I put out all the press kits and all that kind of stuff.

It's extremely difficult I would say to direct and produce because the producer's hat tells you that you have x-amount of time, x-amount of resources, x-amount of money, and x-amount of crew. You have to coordinate to make it work the best logistically and financially. And then as the director you think, "Well I want it to look like this, and I want this many lights, and I want it to have this kind of set design, and we need this much time to get an excellent dolly shot." And so you've got the two things. I did it really well because I felt like I knew what my limits were in terms of willingness to spend time and money in order to have the best artistic quality. Yet at the same time I also knew that cutting the script in half was the kind of decision making where it was either cut the script down so we can have a completed film, or we can shoot half a film and that's it.

I think directing is the harder part. Producing is kind of easier. If you're good at administrating and organizing it doesn't sap your creative energy to do that. It's just a process and you go through it. And then there are other people who, because they are not organized people or administrative people, probably find that the directing side of it is easier because they just don't want to fool with producing at all. I really enjoyed doing both. I think that if I were to direct another film I would find somebody to produce it. Now that I've done it, I would know what I'm looking for. I would actively seek somebody to produce the film, based on certain criteria. Maybe I would have a line producer to be on the set and then an executive producer to be in charge of the money for a feature length film. But at the same time I would love to produce a film for somebody else who is directing because I think I could do a really good job without having to concentrate on the creative part of it.

I think the main thing that is important as an independent director is to really understand what you're getting into because it's not cheap and it's not easy and I've seen a lot of people bite off more than they can chew. There's a guy in Atlanta who has done twelve minutes of a feature on 35mm, and he's in debt on five credit cards and he's not going to finish it. Another friend of mine has eighteen minutes of a feature film and he's totally in debt—his is 35mm also. He's had people interested in buying the film once it's finished, but they aren't willing to put up money toward finishing, so now he's got a really good script and no means for raising the money. Even though directing the feature film is a huge undertaking, the main thing is the money—if you have the money behind you, you can suffer through whatever in order to get it finished.

On Jim's advice we did a short. I couldn't imagine doing a feature

Director Traci Carroll rehearses a scene with actors Lauri Faggioni and Kim Jürgen.

because I had a realistic view of how much time and how much money a feature film would cost. I felt that if I could just get a short film done, then I would know what I was doing. I would have some contacts whom I could call. I would have something to show people what I could do. Then maybe there would be a possibility that I could shoot a feature film in the future. But I think there're some people that want to do the film and want to be famous, and they get into something that can't be finished. Or they get it into the can, and they don't have enough money to cut it or get their final print made—it exists only on video.

One of the challenges was that even though Brian, Jim, and I all have great respect for each other's work and we all ultimately had the same vision for the film, we definitely had our points of friction. And because it was my film and Brian's film, I think it was difficult for Brian to have Jim playing such a large role in the production of the film. But he was the one who had all the experience, and I really trusted that he would not let us do a film that sucked. I really put a lot of faith in him that he knew what he was doing and that he was going to make it look good and that if he had reservations, he would say, "I don't know about this." So we had moments of friction between the three of us when we had this little triangle where one or the other of us was at odds with somebody else, so that was a little difficult.

But I think a lot of partnerships dissolve, and sometimes the film doesn't get finished because people have creative differences. I can say that all through this, we all had creative differences at one point or another, but we were all really dedicated to putting our differences aside and finishing the film and maintaining our personal relationships with each other. We were friends and we didn't want to be like the filmmakers you hear about that had these great partnerships until they did one film together and had creative differences, and now they don't speak. We really didn't want that.

I would definitely like to direct a feature film, and right now I would like to be the writer of the film that I'm directing. Obviously it can't be what our short film is because if you're going to have a feature, you can't make it so abstract that at the end of two hours people have no idea what they've seen. It would definitely have to be more of a story, but I would still like it to have those qualities—not everything is explained to the audience and the audience has to make certain judgments about the characters or situations that are more personal for them. So I would like to write and direct a feature film. And in working on this film I've realized how much money is out there for a good script. So right now I'm focusing on really finding what I think is a good story. I've rewritten thousands of pages and, even though I have a couple stories I like, they're not the one I'm going to marry and spend five years and $500,000 on.

A first feature has to be much more exceptional than anything you do after that because it sort of makes you or breaks you as far as being able to do something else. I'm not going to rush to do another film because I want it to be the right story and the right film and with enough money to hire people and pay them. Doing a short with people that don't know what they're doing and letting them have experience instead of money is great and perfect for a short film. But I'm preparing myself for a thirty-to sixty-day shoot, and you have to have a crew that knows what they're doing and is up to speed the first day that you walk on-set and is really behind what you're shooting. I'm focusing on the story right now. I feel like if it's good enough, the money and the right people will attach to the project because I've seen that happen. I know it's a possibility.

As far as producing I would love to produce a film. But it's difficult because I feel like if I'm going to dedicate the time to do a feature film I'd like it to be one that I'm directing. And unfortunately if you're going to be a full-time producer it takes the same amount of time, and I'm not going to quit my job to produce somebody else's film in the same way that I might be willing to quit my job to direct my own film. But I probably will serve in some producing capacity on the feature that I do because I think it's going to have to be, at least in the beginning, me who sells the film to other people to get them excited about it, to get them on board, and to get them to put their money behind it.

I think everybody likes the idea of having studio backing, whether they admit it or not. It certainly makes it easier, but the flip side of that is that if you have studio backing, usually they're picking the scripts for you, and you're just attached as a director or producer. You don't get to make your love-child film that you would as an independent. Obviously if I'm going to do a feature film it's going to be an independent film because nobody's going to back me now. If I were offered the possibility—if somebody loved whatever feature film I had completed—sure I'd take the money and see what they had to offer. Because even if you direct a terrible script for a studio, you learn so much about how that process works by being on the inside of that system.

As far as my plans, I have looked at several feature length scripts for my next project, but so far, I have not found anything I'm really in love with yet. In a lot of ways, especially for a first feature, and an independent one at that, I think it is really important to find a great script—one that you love as a director, but also one that you let other people read and they love as well. When you're asking people to give one-and-one-half to

151

two hours of their time to watch something you've made, it's very important to tell a good story, and you can't do that without a good script.

I'm not going to rush the process. I see a lot of filmmakers who are so eager to get that first feature out there that they cut a lot of corners in the initial writing, planning, and visualization processes. What they don't realize is that there are so many projects out there (independent and studio) that unless you take the time to build a solid foundation for your work and are willing to spend the time and money to do it right, no one is going to be interested in buying it anyway.

David Zeiger

Why did I do *Displaced in the New South*? Because what really struck me about the immigrant communities in Georgia was that their very existence was subversive in the South. In this very introverted culture—it's the only part of the country that considers itself to have its own culture—it's indigenous or claims to be indigenous. And here you have these people that just sort of plop down—simply their existence screws with that, and I think it's not so much people being ignored as it is people who are out of bounds or are considered to be out of bounds. I like subverting mainstream ideas and mainstream thinking and showing people the uncomfortable things that you can get into. I get a kick out of that.

At the same time I know with *The Band,* the personal element to making it was so strong. I'm not sure if I would necessarily stay in that vein. There are projects that I'm looking at that are in that kind of vein—there's a personal element to it that starts from my personal experience, my family experience, and branches out into something that really has a significance to the world. I like doing personal documentaries—I really liked doing *The Band.* But it's a limited medium. It's not like you can stay with that format for everything—then it can get self-indulgent. There are a lot of people that think that, in their own right, personal documentaries are self-indulgent. They just don't like them because of that.

Question: You find groups that are ignored or overlooked by society. And you have a knack for blending with those groups and telling their

Some of the trombone section from *The Band*.

© 1998 Displaced LLC. Photo by Mike Kandrach.

story in a nonconfrontational and understanding way. Is that a conscious decision or has it just evolved?

It kind of evolved but there is a lot of consciousness. For example, even the whole thing about being nonconfrontational. This was true with both films, *Displaced* and *The Band*. I really enjoy being able to present something in a way that seems very friendly but there's an undercurrent there that you definitely need to realize. When you think about it, you realize there's a sharper edge to it, and I think personally that that's one of the reasons *The Band* hasn't done well in festivals because a lot of those people don't get that. They don't see beyond the gentleness of it. It's true—I was being very consciously gentle and drawing the audience in because I want people to see this in a way so that it does slowly challenge their own thinking and way of acting. I don't think I started that way, but a lot of what I'm trying to do is look at what would be interesting to me to film. I tend to not be a huge fan of documentaries because I like films more that work on an emotional level—that subvert thinking and do it in a subtle way—and not so much films that hit you over the head. I don't find that entertaining, and the medium is an entertainment medium—it's hard to think of it in any other way.

I want to do documentaries because I think what I'm good at is forging entertaining good stories out of real life. I'm not sure that I'm good at making up stories—in fact, I don't think I'm all that good at it. So mainly I do want to stick with documentaries because I think that's where my strength is, and it takes a long time to learn to actually go with your strength rather than what you'd rather do. On the other hand, I think I know what makes a good narrative film. I know what makes a narrative film good for me, and I would love to make a narrative film like that. So right now I'm working on a screenplay based on *The Band*.

The idea of the screenplay is that the father in that film is a guy who has pretty much given up on life and has gone through a lot of similar things that I went through but has reached a point where he isn't really living anymore—he's just existing. He's a wedding photographer and has a not-bad but not-great relationship with his son, and he goes to a football game at his son's high school one day like I did and sees his son being a completely different person in his own world. The father is kind of mesmerized by that and confused by it. He starts spying on his son and actually starts sneaking around to try to see his son's world in a way that he can't as a parent. He actually starts devising really elaborate ways of spying on his son. The change that happens is that the father rediscovers life by living vicariously in his son's world. I'm not too far in terms of what happens in the son's world. I think the story will be fairly similar to Danny and Mary Ellen's story. Part of my difficulty with that, again, is this is all based on what really happened.

Part of the difficulty for me—it's very hard for me—is it's a real challenge to create characters and write dialogue that is better than what is actually there in the documentary. Part of the thing is, and this is unfortunate but I think it's true, is that there's a much bigger audience for narrative film and you can do things in narrative film that you can't do in documentary. Certain things are not considered to be appropriate in a documentary. One of the things that bothers me about the response *The*

Band is getting in festivals is that I think if *The Band* were a narrative film, festivals would love it, but because it's a documentary, a lot of festivals don't deem things that happen in it appropriate. They want documentaries to be hard-hitting and edgier and that kind of thing, but I think their standards for narrative film are much more open. So yes, I do want to continue in documentary because I do believe that's what I'm good at, but I do want to try my hand at narrative. I'm working on the screenplay, and if I'm able to write a screenplay that I think is really good then I'm going to try to make the film.

I am writing it by myself but I'm not going to keep writing it by myself—I want to find a writing partner. I think the ideal situation for me would be to find a writing partner who I have a strong connection with but who would be very good at writing dialogue.

I don't think I could function in the studio-system situation. I just hope I can maintain my independent status. I hope I don't get sucked into the glamour of Hollywood—that's something that scares me enough. I'm not the strongest person in the world—if a certain opportunity comes up I could halfway see myself falling into it, but I do hope to maintain as much independence as possible. On the other hand, one of my main heroes is John Sayles, and he is considered to be one of the great filmmakers. He is very independent but also works to a certain degree within the studio system. He does work-for-hire. I would be perfectly willing to do work-for-hire for television or whatever. That's what John Sayles does, and then he makes his films through the money he's able to make that way and through the contacts that he makes and that kind of stuff. I'd love to someday learn more about how he works. So I think it's wrong to say, "Oh absolutely not. I have to maintain my purity." I guess I do want to maintain my independence and I guess in a certain sense I'm too old to not do that, but I don't know.

As an independent filmmaker you have to be able to accept rejection because—this isn't my quote I heard someone say this and it's really true—the only constant in independent film is rejection. When you get rejected all the time by all kinds of people, you have to be able to go through that and still maintain your willingness to push on. Another thing you have to do is you have to be obsessive—you have to be able to get so obsessed with the project that you're willing to go through no one else giving a crap about it. And you have to be willing to make it no matter whether you can raise the money or not and find the ways to do that. You have to be so determined that you'll make it no matter what obstacles you run up against because you run up against tremendous obstacles. If your attitude is going to be, "Well I need $150,000 to make this movie and when I raise $150,000 then I'll make it," then you'll never make it.

Obviously you've got to believe that what you are doing is worth doing. It's a very ego-driven life. You have to believe you're doing good work even if no one else thinks your work is good. On the other hand, I think you have to be willing to listen to people who disagree with you or who don't think that what you're doing is all that good. That's a big problem because it's so ego driven. I love screenings because you get feedback, but unfortunately the people who loved the film talk and the people who didn't love it don't say anything. So you don't get that kind of constructive criticism. I feel that you need to be willing to listen to people who don't like what you're doing—not who don't like it but who have criticism—and take those criticisms for what they are and learn from them. And I think a lot of filmmakers don't do that. It's a hard thing to do because you put so much of your heart and soul into it. I've had people from the documentary film world say they didn't like *The Band* because they didn't like the personal approach. There's one person in particular who said, "If I were making the film I would take you out altogether and make it just about the kids," so you have to listen to that and ask, is there something there? Is there something to that? And do you toss it out or do you say, "Okay, there's a point to that." In this case my conclusion to that was, "Fine, you make a film"—this person has never made a film in his life. You have to take them for what they're worth.

I think what makes me want to continue is the challenge—how hard it is to do. And if you are able to successfully make a film that you are happy with and that connects with audiences I can't think of a better accomplishment artistically. It's just got that personal satisfaction for me even though it includes a tremendous amount of pain. I guess that's part of what makes it worthwhile—it's not the money—not for independent documentary film. It's very hard to make money on that. A guy told me when I was making *Displaced* that he had made a film called *Banned in the USA,* and that it was a fairly successful documentary film. He said that a successful documentary film is one where you can pay off all your debts and have a little bit of money to start your next film. It's a really rare documentary that makes money. Even the ones that get a lot of screen time don't make much money.

The Band was broadcast in the United States on the PBS series *POV* in 1998, and in 2000 it will have its European premier on the La Sept Arte Network in France and Germany.

I am now back at high school, producing and directing a series called *Senior Year* that will air on PBS. With six recent film school graduates, I am following a dozen seniors at FairFax High School, the most culturally diverse public school in Los Angeles (and, coincidentally, my alma mater from back in the not-so-diverse days). In the wake of the near hysteria about teenagers and teen culture that followed the Columbine shootings, *Senior Year* will present the world as teens themselves see and live in it. It will be broadcast as a series, and in 1999 it received a major grant from the Corporation for Public Broadcasting for its production.

Chris Blasingame

As a producer/director, you have to let things roll off you. When the credit card people call you up and call you a bunch of names you have to call them a bunch of names back and tell them to screw off. I wouldn't wish it on anybody else because it's not fun. You just have to let things roll off your back. The poverty level sucks. I wouldn't wish it on anybody, but then again if you have to do it you have to do it. But it's getting old. I'm married—I'd love a house; I'd love kids, but I can't. I want to soon. But it gets to be depressing. When I was twenty-five it didn't

(From right) Director Chris Balsingame works with Mark Yoder and Chad Outler on the streets of Towanda. Photo by Tim Sabo.

matter so much, but now I'm getting a little old to be living this lifestyle. But you've got to let things roll off your back.

I don't have any respect for money. I don't come from an extremely rich family or anything. I grew up pretty middle class and poor. I just don't have respect for money. It's bad. It wouldn't be so bad if I were by myself, but now I'm married, and we keep our finances separate. I'm holding my weight, but I just feel like I should be a little more responsible. But if I was, I wouldn't be doing this, so I don't know what the answer is.

You have to be a gambler—you have to be a total gambler—you can't be scared to spend money, even money you don't have. But you've got to make things happen, and you have to do it without anything sometimes. And I think I'm good at all those things—the gambling and letting things roll off your back and spending money. I don't think I ever had a problem with those things. I have no respect for money, which is one of my biggest criticisms of myself.

I think you have to be able to see the whole picture. You have to know the story like the back of your hand and you have to want to tell the story. You can't be written in stone about things because you're working with people. You're working with human beings, and you've got to get them in the process. You can't say, "Say the line like this." You've got to make everybody feel like they're contributing, and they are—it's not a lie.

I always like to say you have to out-dumb people, which goes against the fact that you have to be the one on the set that everyone can turn to. But you have to know what you want by letting people think it's their idea, and it is their idea. You can't overpower people. And you have to be nurturing to people throughout the whole process. You have to hold the reins but you have to hold them really loosely. You know where you want to go with it and you have to guide it there, but you can't force it there. It's a weird little play between things to get what you want.

A lot of good things happen that aren't expected, but a lot of bad things also happen and you go down the wrong road. On *Roadrunner* I let it go where it organically went, and we didn't go down any bad roads, and that's a good thing. We didn't go down any roads that were awful and that made us think, "Oh how did we get down here?" We let it happen. I guess you have to have the big picture and plan, and you have to have your thoughts well organized. You have to know every aspect of what's going on. And you have to let problems roll off you. Say there's a problem with equipment and you have to get that shot but it's not the shot you wanted. Well, too bad. The great thing about producing/directing is the money I put together, so I'm responsible and I'm not going to be a real crybaby when I don't get what I want. In fact I'm more than happy to cut things. It's fun. I don't have people telling me, "You can't do this—there's no way you can do this." I'm the first one that says that. Because I know what I can do for a certain amount of money, and I was pretty close to it. I'm not demanding things I know I can't have. I'm responsible for people and money on this.

I might get a producer if I found somebody I really really dug for a producer, but I'd rather keep it close to my chest. But yeah, bring in people you work well with and you work closely with and you trust. Trust is such a big part of it. If I have a weird, bad feeling about somebody, that usually means no.

Film is an art, and I don't think I'm a great artist or anything, and I don't intend to be, but it's too expensive to screw around with. I don't think it's a form for your personal mental masturbation so I always want to make something that's going to make money. I don't want to make an epic movie that has a small audience. And that's fine because sometimes I want to make a movie that does have a small audience but I won't expect to spend a lot of money on it.

I would love the money and the support of the studio system but I mostly want control because I want my films to be exactly what I want them to be. I don't want to go making films that I intended to be one thing and then a bunch of people got their hands in it and changed it. I don't want to have to take on a star or an actor that I don't think is appropriate for the role just because they have a certain amount of points in Hollywood and I'm doing it for money. And on down the line when I have enough films under my belt where I have some kind of reputation to back up my filmmaking then I would go into the studio system and hopefully not be pushed around. But I don't really want to get in there, make films for them, and not have any control. I have a respect for the money that goes into filmmaking—I don't take it for granted at all. But as much as filmmaking is a collaborative process with other people—it's got to be—it has to be one person's voice. I think one person has to be a little Napoleon about it. And I don't think you get that when you are new in the studio system.

Lately I don't see many great films come out of the studio system, and I wonder when they're going to make the next *Chinatown.* Who does have the power to do that? I don't know. I just keep thinking, "When is the next great movie going to come out?" I liked Sam Raimi's latest film a lot and I like a lot of independents. I liked *Shakespeare in Love,* too. But when is the next truly great movie going to be made? It's usually because its authorship is a vision of a strong director who doesn't have to put up with a lot of outside influences. Who has that anymore? I don't know. I

160

can't stand the fact that all these films that are being made are probably bastardized versions of what they were intended to be because of test audiences and all that other crap.

I basically want to make dark movies, but I don't go to see a lot of dark movies. I love *Bad Lieutenant* and all those Abel Ferrara movies, but I would love to make funny movies—I want to make comedies. I don't want to show *Roadrunner* to many people until the sound is set, but I do show it to a few people, and the great thing is that people are laughing. And also they're hating Liz. But it's great because when I'm thinking, "Oh this doesn't work and what's wrong with this and it's a big mess," people are watching it and hating Liz, which is good. They're loving *Roadrunner,* which is good. It's exactly what I planned. And they're laughing. And that's great because I meant for it to be darkly funny. That's good.

Actually the premise of the film that I initially came up with may not be the strongest point in the movie anymore, but the movie is something in itself now, and that happened by letting it go where it wanted to go. When I get more experience I'll be able to get it more where I want it to be, but that's where it is now, and it's in the ballpark of where I want it to be. When I go back and look at where I wanted it to be and the message behind it, it's not so much about that anymore. It's about something else, which is interesting and fun. I let it go there and I'm fine with that.

I'd love to do documentaries. I watch a lot of documentaries—I watch a lot of nature documentaries and biographies. I'm a sucker for that kind of stuff, especially with the great channels that are on now. But I am worried about trying to find a story. I think there's a trend now of people trying to find a dramatic story in something that's not so dramatic. They try to find some point where every rock star fell and came back from. Well that's sort of being irresponsible. I would love to make a documentary but I'm worried what would be expected. I shouldn't be worried—I should just go make a film and have people take it or leave it. But the situation of documentaries does concern me because you can't make a totally objective documentary. You still have to point the camera at something. I think we're being irresponsible by

focusing on certain aspects of people's lives to make them more commercial. I would like to make one, but if I was hired to make one I think
I'd have a problem if somebody asked me to do something that manip-
ulated the story, although I know you have to do it to some degree
sometime. As much as I enjoy watching them, I have a problem with
VH-1 rockumentaries—the "he had an addiction to cough syrup and
almost lost everything but rebounded strongly" thing. So I would love
to do documentaries, but if I was hired to do them I would have to let
the subject unfold and be as natural as possible and try to keep the
subjectivity to a minimum.

I would help anybody out with any project, but I'm not looking to
find a job in film anymore. I need to expand as a producer and the only
way I'm going to do that is by seeing these things through further. In the
long run I'm better off not going to film school. I wish I had gotten some
degree—I wish I had the foresight to become a lawyer who wanted to
make films. I don't think there's anything more powerful. What is a producer? What is anybody? I think it all comes down to having legal savvy.
It's all experience I'm gaining. I wish I had done something like that, but
I just wanted to make films when I was in college and when I was that
age—I wasn't thinking down the road. But I think the only good reason
to get a film degree is if you want to become a film historian or something like that. I don't think it's totally necessary.

I will probably have a project to do this summer—something small so
I can keep doing it. I want to shoot *Cold Ground* during the winter of 2000.

I do have some realizations about what it takes to make independent
films. You have to jump—you have to jump all the time, blindly, because
it won't get done if you don't. You have to be extremely prepared, but be
very loose at the same time and let things happen.

It's better to be a big fish in a little pool than a little fish in a big pool.
That's why I won't try to go out to L.A. to make it until I have enough
things under my belt. It doesn't appeal to me to try to go out and hus-
tle scripts in Hollywood. I can't understand people who talk about doing
that, especially when they're nobodies. I can't stress enough—your script

is not going to sell, and you're a nobody. The only way you're going to get the script made is if you pick it up and do it yourself. And to do that is a lot of sacrifice. And if you're not ready to do that then why are you doing it in the first place?

Everybody wants to be a screenwriter. I wouldn't even insult writers by calling myself a writer. I have ideas and I write my ideas. I don't have the discipline. I don't read a lot—I don't do a lot of things that I should if I want to be a real writer. I read manuals on how to work certain cameras and how to enter things in festivals. I'm not a writer. Actually I like it that way because I don't want to write something because it's the same story as something else. I just like my ideas. I'm a director. I can't work for somebody else. I can't. So I'm screwed if I can't get this thing to work. I don't know what else to do.

Why climb the ladder when you can walk through the door? You see some of these movies and you wonder what they had to do to be forty years old and finally direct a movie in the studio system. And it's not necessarily a good movie either. I don't think it's a system that's conducive to a lot of things. Remember in the early seventies and early sixties with Spielberg and Coppola, and then there were the new filmmakers like Coen and Jim Jarmusch. Who is it now?

There are the fake independents who look low budget, but the studios give them the money and the luxury and star power, so they're really not independent. They are sort of made within the studio system in a way. I try to understand if you worked and lived within the industry how weird the rest of the world must seem to you. You're living within a false, weird, strange world that doesn't really relate to the rest of the world. That's why being too inbred in Hollywood is not a good thing. You have to get your drive and inspiration from outside Hollywood to break that pattern.

What am I doing now? Working off debt and enjoying luxuries like health insurance. But I am getting ready to do it all over again. I plan on shooting another short in the summer of 2000 called *Lucky Man* and then a feature in the winter called *Cold Ground*.

163

Chad Etchison

I know that I have so much to learn and I'm still very much a beginning filmmaker, but I think I know what you have to have to do it. I think that's what I got from this project. It's a massive undertaking. It is unbelievable. I definitely got bathed in fire. I think I went through everything you could go through—I think we made a really good film, and I think I learned a lot, which are the two things I wanted to do. I wanted to see if I could do it because I wasn't sure. Everybody told me I was crazy, so I thought, "Well let's see if I can do this." I've always had the attitude that if I want to do something then I'm going to do it, and I don't care what anybody says. Sometimes that's a cool attitude but sometimes you may not be able to do it.

I had some fun. It's such a hard thing. It was fun, but it was not fun. It's hard to say because at times I would think this is the greatest, the most fun, especially when I was acting. That really was fun. I would qualify that as fun. Some of the directing moments and some of the producing hassles I can't even describe. It is the worst—you just want to go crawl under something and hide. I've never done anything that made me feel like this. It was so hard and that's what's hard to explain to somebody—if you're going to do this be ready for the most pain, and it's that self-inflicted pain. It wasn't really that much fun, to be honest. It was fun but it wasn't like a vacation is fun or like even if you're working somewhere and it gets fun for a moment. It's not like that. I was always looking toward the end and I thought, "When this is over I'm going to be happy as hell." But in the weirdest way as soon as it was over I was ready to go again. It may be like childbirth—it sucks the whole way through, but when you make it, you forget and you're ready to go again.

I would love to be a real director and get paid by somebody. That would be fabulous. But I know that whatever level you attain, you want more. Like right now, most people would kill to make a film like I just did. It's been hell to raise the money—that was torture. I put my wife through hell and I put myself through hell, but I don't have to hear anything from anybody. I did exactly what I wanted to do and that was that.

164

Chad Etchison directs Shannon Young in *The Initiate*. © 2000 Etch-Me Films. Photo by P. Daniel Maughon.

Right now I'm doing exactly what I want to do. Nobody can come in and say, "Hey make this a little more Generation X." Nobody's going to do that to me.

But if you're hired by the studios then the money's everything to them—they don't give a damn about art. That has nothing to do with the equation. If you can make art and it makes money then you're a great artist. If it doesn't make money then you're a loser—that's how they think. That's understandable if you're in their shoes; it's all understandable; it's just painful. When you're in their shoes, they're putting the money on the table, and they're having to sell it to guys in Iowa or wherever.

If I did another one like this I would probably act—it's too hard to pass up. I don't know if it's ego or what it is, but I love acting. That's what I did first. I think that I'm one of those weird people who will always try to do that.

My scripts may be totally lame and that may mean I make mediocre films all my life, but I really like the idea where you come up with the concept and maybe find a collaborator, somebody who's a super great screenwriter, and maybe work with him. But I really like the idea of me

165

Initiate crew member Tripp Norton sets a light during the bar scene. © 2000 Etch-Me Films. Photo by P. Daniel Maughon.

thinking of everything and keeping a real heavy hand in the project. I really think that's the kind of director I want to be.

I want to learn more about lighting and cinematography. I don't want to be the guy who's shooting it, but I want to know what Jim's doing every minute and why. Now that I know so much more about cinematography I can do so much more with my shots. I can even know what kind of lens I'm going to use. When I was storyboarding I didn't know what kind of lens I was going to use. I had no idea. I had no clue. I would say, "Well here I want it to be a close-up," and we'd draw a picture of the close-up. And I would ask, "Well, what lens will we use?" And Jim would say, "Oh we'll probably use an 85 or 100." And then you would actually sometimes choose it on the set. Now I can actually say, "I think I want to use an 85 there or a 100 there." Now I know. I want to get better at that. When you listen to Ridley Scott do his director's commentary, like on *G.I. Jane,* that guy knows everything. For one thing, he can operate the camera probably better than whoever is running the camera. He knows lighting—he has very distinctive ideas about lighting—he's a super genius guy. I want to get to that point. I don't know if I ever will, but I don't want to be like, "Oh yeah I directed a film—I hung out." I want to be part of the whole process.

My wife, Mary, and I formed Etch-Me Films in 1997 to produce independent feature films that I could both write and direct. As of February 2000, we are relocating Etch-Me Films to Los Angeles, and a new film is in the initial planning phases.

Appendix

Director/Producer's Survival Kit

Now for the part they don't cover in class. If you're one of those totally together people who never suffers from panic attacks or disorganization or fatigue or low blood sugar, then you don't need to read any further. But if you're not perfect and you want to minimize any potentially unsavory dramatics of your own on the set (tantrums and being unprepared don't look good for you as director), we've come up with a survival kit of sorts. We polled filmmakers to ask them what their must-haves are on the set. The following is a checklist of filmmakers' first aid.

- Boxes of energy bars and granola bars. Good quick energy that doesn't require refrigeration. Stops the stomachs from growling when catering is delayed and delayed and delayed.
- Really comfortable shoes and a change of socks. Dry socks are essential in the event of tsunamis or river crossings. Wet feet are no fun.
- Your own stash of bottled water. And plenty of it. Dehydration does not make for a good director.

- Tylenol or Advil in bulk for when your muscles or your head go into revolt mode.
- Lists of all the phone numbers you could possibly need (all crew, rental houses, local film commission, locations, etc.).
- By the way, if you care about anything on paper, laminate it because it will get soaked, if not by rain then by spilled drinks.
- Quarters for the phone when the cell-phone battery goes dead or you're in a dead zone.
- Copies of every permit and contract you have in case the local authorities arrive.
- Pens and paper. You will need them.
- Extra toilet paper/paper towels.
- Wet wipes or hand cleanser. Trust us on this.
- Plastic garbage bags by the gross. Good for trash; emergency duvateen, covering white carpet to prevent stains when your gooey special effect goes awry; tying stuff together; and emergency rain gear.
- More energy bars and granola bars.
- Toothbrush and toothpaste.
- If not tooth care products, then at least chewing gum or Altoids.
- Pocket knife, Leatherman, or some multi-purpose tool.
- Extra clothespins—there are never enough.
- Gaffer tape—you'll be surprised how many places this comes in handy.
- String—you never know.
- If you wear contacts, bring saline solution—no one ever seems to have it.
- If you're shooting outside, bring a small radio to catch weather reports.
- Ditto for a raincoat.
- Extra energy bars and granola bars—picking up on a theme here?
- Certificates for free dinners to pass out to outstanding benefactors or contributors on any given day. These are also good to boost

crew morale when they've had a particularly hard day—they're just as important if not more important than the actors.

·   A pocket full of cash in small bills for unforeseen expenses and emergencies.

·   Copies of any positive press you've received so if anyone gets restless or challenges your project, they can be assured that the ship is indeed in good hands.

·   Yes, energy bars again—it can be a long drive home.

Discounts/Deals for Independent Filmmakers

Many national and local equipment rental and production services offer discounts or deals for independent projects. Your best bet is to simply call each establishment you're interested in doing business with, explain your project and its status, and ask if they could work with you. Many outfits will work out deals on an individual basis. Some have standard discounts for independents.

For example, Mole-Richardson Co. gives discounts in their studio depot store to independent/student/low-budget filmmakers and offers deals to these individuals on rentals. You can visit their stores online at the following sites:

·   *www.Mole.com*
·   *www.StudioDepot.com*
·   *www.Moletown.com*
·   *www.StudioAuctions.com*

Other companies support filmmakers indirectly. Avid Technologies donates Avid editing systems to community-based nonprofits that support local filmmakers. Two specific examples are donations to the Boston Film + Video Foundation and the San Francisco Film Arts Foundation. Filmmakers can rent out editing suites for as low as $25 per hour. Both foundations also have supported the Sundance Institute with several high-end systems for their summer program.

Support is available. You just have to do the research and initiate the conversation.

Film Schools

If you are considering a traditional film school education, the top six internationally recognized full-time film programs dedicated to producing film and television are all in the United States.

Formalized film school education is typically offered at colleges and universities. Well over two hundred university and college film schools in the United States alone offer bachelor's degrees in film. Over thirty-five schools offer master's degrees, and a smaller handful offer doctoral degrees. Untold thousands enroll in bachelor-level filmmaking classes each year. In the more elite echelons of master's degree schooling, the numbers are still impressive. The top seven American master's programs annually enroll around 270 new students and at any given time have about 830 students in their programs. They are, in alphabetical order:

- American Film Institute, tel: 323/856-7628, *www.afionline.org*
- California Institute of the Arts, tel: 805/253-7825, *www.calarts.edu*
- Columbia University, School of the Arts, Film Division, tel: 212/854-2815, *www.columbia.edu/cu.arts/*
- Florida State University, Graduate Film Conservatory, tel: 850/644-0453, *www.fsu.edu/~film*
- New York University, Department of Film and Television, Graduate Division, tel: 212/998-1918, *www.nyu.edu/tisch/cinema/*
- University of California, Los Angeles, School of Theater, Film and Television, tel: 310/825-8787, *www.filmtv.ucla.edu*
- University of Southern California, School of Cinema-Television, tel: 213/740-8358, *www.cntv.usc.edu*

Film Workshops

Should you choose not to go the traditional film school route for formal education, we have found that shorter programs such as film workshops can offer valuable experience and contacts for a fraction of the cost and time investment. There are several hundred workshops in the United States that offer programs and courses in film production such as:

- The International Film and Television Workshops, *www.meworkshops.com/filmworkshops/index2.html,* toll-free: 877/577-7700 or tel: 207/236-8581, fax: 207/236-2558, e-mail: *info@ MEWorkshops.com*
- The Motion Picture Pro Course, *www.pipeline.com/~rrdirect,* tel: 212/691-7791, fax: 212/352-2728, e-mail: *MPPC@pipeline.com*
- Hollywood Film Institute 2-Day Film School, *www.hollywoodu. com/2daycc.htm,* toll-free: 800/366-3456 (United States only) or tel: 323/933-3456, fax: 323/933-1464, e-mail: *filmschool@hollywoodu. com*
- Millennium Film Workshop, tel: 212/673-0090
- New York Film Academy, tel: 212/674-4300, *www.nyfa.com*
- Writers Boot Camp, toll-free: 800/800-1733
- Full Sail, toll-free: 800/226-7625, *www.fullsail.com*
- University of Southern California, School of Cinema-Television Summer Production Workshop, tel: 213/740-1742, *hjttpa://cinema-tv.usc.edu/spw/*

Universities such as Princeton, Yale, and the New York Film Academy also offer film programs for aspiring high school filmmakers. Media-related companies like Avid, makers of nonlinear editing software and hardware, are joining that movement.

Internet Newsgroups for Filmmakers

A newsgroup is a bulletin board of sorts on which you can post messages for the Internet community to read and respond to. They are a great way to reach the masses. As a matter of fact, we found some of our interviewees via the newsgroups. Many people use them to exchange information, sell equipment, or just as a forum for their comments and opinions. Refer to your browser's online help for specific information on how to use the newsgroups.

Here is a list of our favorite film and video-related newsgroups:

- *rec.arts.movies.production*
- *alt.movies.visual-effects*
- *alt.movies.cinematography*
- *alt.movies.hitchcock*
- *www.altfilm.com*
- *misc.writing.screenplays*
- *rec.arts.movies.tech*
- *alt.movies.independent*
- *rec.video.production*
- *rec.video.desktop*
- *rec.video.professional*

Internet Listserv Groups for Filmmakers

A listserv group is the best way to reach a specific group of people. It's sort of like having a personal team of experts at your disposal.

For example, suppose you had a question about desktop video editing. You would send your e-mail question to a listserv computer that would then distribute your e-mail to everyone who had subscribed to that particular desktop video list. Anyone who wanted to answer your question would either send it back to the listserv, once again distributing your question and the new response, or they could contact you directly. Many times, a question may spark an ongoing discussion between subscribers. Tech support technicians for the big boys like Avid, Media 100, and Adobe are known to be ardent players in these discussions.

Some helpful listserv groups we've found are:

- *bit.listserv.cinema-l*
- *bit.listserv.film-l*
- *bit.listserv.script-l*

Film Festival Web Sites

Film festivals abound for independent films, short and feature length. Many festivals are geared to specific types and genres of film, so it is worth doing your research to pick festivals best suited to your work. And, of course, you should keep an updated calendar of festival submission deadlines, requirements, and dates. These Web sites follow film festivals of all kinds and will help you get started on your research:

·   *filmfestivals.com/*
·   *marklitwak.com/filmfes.htm*
·   *film.com/watch/nb_trailers.dyn*

Film Software Web Sites

Computer technology has infiltrated and profoundly altered what was once the sole domain of old-school filmmakers. Although we pray to the old-school great ones regularly and respect their innovations in film, new technology is also a good thing. Here are some sites that offer a multitude of exciting software applications for old-school and cutting-edge filmmakers alike:

·   Film Profit, *www.filmprofit.com/*
·   The Writer's Store (formerly the Writer's Computer Store), *writerscomputer.com*
·   Filmmaker Software, *www.filmmakersoftware.com*

Film Commissions

Film commissions can be tremendously beneficial in paving the way to a smoother production. There are a few things you can do, however, to facilitate your relationship with your film commission friends. When looking for locations, give plenty of lead time, so they can best respond to your requests. Along with that, the better informed the film commission is about your project, the better able they will be to help your production. This can include providing them with a script breakdown and as many details about location shoots as possible. Good film commissions not only work with you but with the community in which you will be shooting to better prepare the locals for what it will mean to shoot a movie in their midst. For instance, if traffic will be affected, the production will run much more smoothly if everyone is advised ahead of time and understands why.

Another tip is to give the local press some time at the beginning of your production. They can be your best friends if you treat them well and give them some time when you start shooting. In this way you prevent any hard feelings with the media and you get some helpful publicity. Also to facilitate favorable public relations, consider the possibility of hiring local crew.

Lastly, remember the film commission when it comes time to say thank you. Put them in your credits. Don't forget the importance of "thank you."

United States Film Commissions

Alabama

Alabama Film Office

401 Adams Avenue

Montgomery, AL 36104

Tel: 800/248-0033; 334/242-0400

Fax: 334/242-2414

Alaska

Alaska Film Office

3601 C Street, Suite 700

Anchorage, AK 99503

Tel: 907/269-8137

Fax: 907/269-8136

Arizona

Apache Junction Chamber of Commerce

P.O. Box 1747

Apache Junction, AZ 85217-1747

Tel: 800/252-3141, 480/982-3141

Fax: 480/982-3234

Arizona Film Commission

3800 N. Central Avenue, Building D

Phoenix, AZ 85012

Tel: 800/523-6695, 602/280-1380

Fax: 602/280-1384

City of Phoenix Motion Picture Office

200 W. Washington, 10th Floor

Phoenix, AZ 85003-1611

Tel: 602/262-4850

Fax: 602/534-2295

City of Prescott

P.O. Box 2059

Prescott, AZ 86302

Tel: 520/445-3500

Fax: 520/776-6255

Cochise County Film Commission
1415 W. Melody Lane, Building B
Bisbee, AZ 85603
Tel: 520/432-9454, 520/432-9200
Fax: 520/432-5016

Greater Flagstaff Economic Council
1300 S. Milton, Suite 125
Flagstaff, AZ 86001
Tel: 800/575-7658, 602/779-7658
Fax: 602/556-0940

Globe Miami Film Commission
1360 N. Broad Street
U.S. 60
P.O. Box 2539
Globe, AZ 85502
Tel: 800/804-5623, 520/425-4495
Fax: 520/425-3410

Holbrook Film Commission
465 N. First Avenue
P.O. Box 70
Holbrook, AZ 86005
Tel: 602/524-6225
Fax: 602/524-2159

Navajo Nation Film Office
P.O. Box 2310
Window Rock, AZ 86515
Tel: 602/871-6656, 602/871-6655
Fax: 602/871-7355

Page/Lake Powell Film Commission
106 S. Lake Powell Boulevard
P.O. Box 727
Page, AZ 86040
Tel: 520/645-2741
Fax: 520/645-3181

Sedona Film Commission
P.O. Box 2489
Sedona, AZ 86339
Tel: 520/204-1123
Fax: 520/204-1064

Scottsdale Film Office
3939 Civic Center Boulevard
Scottsdale, AZ 85251
Tel: 602/994-2636
Fax: 602/994-7780

Tucson Film Office
166 W. Almeda Street
Tucson, AZ 85701
Tel: 520/791-4000, 520/429-1000
Fax: 520/791-4963

Wickenburg Film Commission
216 N. Frontier Street
P.O. Drawer CC
Wickenburg, AZ 85358
Tel: 520/684-5479
Fax: 520/684-5470

Yavapai Film Commission

309 E. Gurley Street

Rescott, AZ 86303

Tel: 520/778-0101

Fax: 520/778-0101

URL:*www.primenet.com/~sherylat/yfc.html*

Yuma Film Commission

P.O. Box 230

Yuma, AZ 85366

Tel: 602/341-1616, 602/782-2567

Fax: 602/343-0038

Arkansas

Arkansas Motion Picture Development

   Office

1 State Capital Mall, Room 2C-200

Little Rock, AR 72201

Tel: 501/682-7676

Fax: 501/682-FILM

Eureka Springs Chamber of Commerce

P.O. Box 551

Eureka Springs, AR 72632

Tel: 501/253-8737

California

California Film Commission

6922 Hollywood Boulevard, Suite 600

Hollywood, CA 90028-6126

Tel: 800/858-4PIX, 213/736-2465

Fax: 213/736-2522

Catalina Island Film Commission

P.O. Box 217

Avalon, CA 90704

Tel: 310/510-7646

Fax: 310/510-1646

Chico Chamber of Commerce

500 Main Street, P.O. Box 3038

Chico, CA 95927

Tel: 916/891-5556, ext. 326

Fax: 916/891-3613

City of Big Bear Lake Film Office

39707 Big Bear Boulevard

P.O. Box 10000

Big Bear Lake, CA 92315

Tel: 909/878-3040

Fax: 909/866-6766

City of Fillmore Film Commission

524 Sespe Avenue

P.O. Box 487

Fillmore, CA 93016

Tel: 805/524-3701

Fax: 805/524-5707

City of Pasadena

100 N. Garfield Avenue, #103

Pasadena, CA 91109

Tel: 818/405-4152

Fax: 818/405-4785

El Dorado/Tahoe Film Commission
542 Main Street
Placerville, CA 95667
Tel: 800/457-6279, 916/626-4400
Fax: 916/642-1624

Eureka-Humboldt County Convention
     and Visitors Bureau
1034 Second Street
Eureka, CA 95501-0541
Tel: 800/346-3482, 707/443-5097,
     800/338-7352 (California only)
Fax: 707/443-5115

Kern County Board of Trade
2101 Oak Street
P.O. Bin 1312
Bakersfield, CA 93302
Tel: 800/500-KERN
Fax: 661/861-2017

Long Beach Office of Special Events
One World Trade Center, Suite 300
Long Beach, CA 90831-0300
Tel: 310/436-7703
Fax: 310/435-5653

Monterey County Film Commission
801 Lighthouse Avenue
P.O. Box 111
Monterey, CA 93942-0111
Tel: 408/646-0910
Fax: 408/655-9244

Motion Picture and Television Division
6922 Hollywood Boulevard, Suite 614
Los Angeles, CA 90028
Tel: 213/461-8614
Fax: 213/847-5009

Orange County Film Office
One City Boulevard West, Suite 401
Orange, CA 92668
Tel: 714/634-2900
Fax: 714/978-0742

Palm Springs Desert Resorts Convention
     and Visitors Bureau/Film Office
69-930 Highway 111, Suite 201
Rancho Mirage, CA 92270
Tel: 760/770-9000, 800/967-3767
Fax: 760/770-9001

Placer County Film Office
13460 Lincoln Way, Suite A
Auburn, CA 95603
Tel: 916/887-2111
Fax: 916/887-2134

Redding Convention and Visitors Bureau
777 Auditorium Drive
Redding, CA 96001
Tel: 800/874-7562, 530/225-4100
Fax: 530/225-4354

Ridgecrest Film Commission
100 W. California Avenue
Ridgecrest, CA 93555
Tel: 800/847-4830, 619/375-8202
Fax: 619/371-1654

Sacramento Area Film Commission
1421 K Street
Sacramento, CA 95814
Tel: 916/264-7777
Fax: 916/264-7788

San Bernardino/Riverside County Film
    Commission
3281 E. Guasti Road, Suite 100
Ontario, CA 91761
Tel: 909/984-3400, ext. 231
Fax: 909/460-7733

San Diego Film Commission
402 W. Broadway, Suite 1000
San Diego, CA 92101-3585
Tel: 619/234-3456
Fax: 619/234-0571

San Francisco Film and Video Arts
    Commission
Mayor's Office
401 Van Ness Avenue, #417
San Francisco, CA 94102
Tel: 415/554-6244
Fax: 415/554-6503

San Jose Film and Video Commission
333 W. San Carlos, Suite 1000
San Jose, CA 95110
Tel: 800/726-5673, 408/295-9600
Fax: 408/295-3937

San Luis Obispo County Film Commission
1041 Chorro Street, Suite E
San Luis Obispo, CA 93401
Tel: 805/541-8000
Fax: 805/543-9498

Santa Clarita SCV Film Liaison Office
23920 Valencia Boulevard, Suite 125
Santa Clarita, CA 91355-2175
Tel: 800/4FILMSC, 805/259-4787
Fax: 805/259-8628

Santa Cruz County Conference and
    Visitors Council
701 Front Street
Santa Cruz, CA 95060
Tel: 408/425-1234
Fax: 408/425-1260

Santa Barbara County Film Council
5390 Overpass Road, Suite F
P.O. Box 92111
Santa Barbara, CA 93190-2111
Tel: 805/962-6668
Fax: 805/969-5960
URL: *www.silcom.com/sbarb/filmservices/
    film.html*

Santa Monica Mountains NRA
30401 Agoura Road, Suite 100
Agoura Hills, CA 91301
Tel: 818/597-1036, ext. 212
Fax: 818/597-8537

Sonoma County Film Liaison Office
5000 Roberts Lake Road, Suite A
Rohnert Park, CA 94928
Tel: 707/586-8100, 707/586-8110
Fax: 707/586-8111

Temecula Valley Film Council
43174 Business Park Drive
Temecula, CA 92590
Tel: 909/699-6267
Fax: 909/694-1999

Colorado
Boulder County Film Commission
P.O. Box 73
Boulder, CO 80306
Tel: 800/444-0447, 303/442-1044
Fax: 303/938-8837

Colorado Motion Picture and TV
   Commission
1625 Broadway, Suite 1700
Denver, CO 80202
Tel: 303/620-4500
Fax: 303/620-4545

Colorado Springs Film Commission
30 S. Nevada Avenue, Suite 405
Colorado Springs, CO 80903
Tel: 719/578-6943
Fax: 719/578-6394

Fremont/Custer County Film Commission
P.O. Box 8
Canon City, CO 81215
Tel: 719/275-5149

Fort Morgan Area Film Commission
710 E. Railroad Avenue
P.O. Box 100
Fort Morgan, CO 80701
Tel: 303/867-3001
Fax: 303/867-3039

Greeley/Weld County Film Commission
902 7th Avenue
Greeley, CO 80631
Tel: 970/352-3566
Fax: 970/352-3572

Mayor's Office of Art, Culture, and Film
280 14th Street
Denver, CO 80202
Tel: 303/640-2686
Fax: 303/640-2737

Trinidad Film Commission
136 W. Main Street
Trinidad, CO 81082
Tel: 800/748-1970, 719/846-9412
Fax: 719/846-4550

Yampa Valley Film Board, Inc.
Box 772305
Steamboat Springs, CO 80477
Tel: 970/879-0882
Fax: 970/879-2543

Connecticut
Connecticut Film, Video, and Media Office
865 Brook Street
Rocky Hill, CT 06067
Tel: 203/258-4339
Fax: 203/529-0535

Danbury Film Office
72 West Street
P.O. Box 406
Danbury, CT 06813
Tel: 800/841-4488, 203/743-0546
Fax: 203/794-1439

Delaware
Delaware Film Office
99 Kings Highway
P.O. Box 1401
Dover, DE 19903
Tel: 800/441-8846, 302/739-4271
Fax: 302/739-5749

District of Columbia
Mayor's Office of Motion Picture and TV
717 4th Street, N.W., 12th Floor
Washington, DC 20005
Tel: 202/727-6600
Fax: 202/727-3787

Florida
Broward/Ft. Lauderdale Film and
    Television Office
200 E. Las Olas Boulevard, Suite 1850
Fort Lauderdale, FL 33301
Tel: 305/524-3113
Fax: 305/524-3167

Central Florida Development Council
600 N. Broadway, #300
P.O. Box 1839
Bartow, FL 33830
Tel: 813/534-4371
Fax: 813/533-1247

Florida Entertainment Commission
505 17th Street
Miami Beach, FL 33139
Tel: 800/716-7770, 305/673-7468

Florida Keys and Key West Film Commission
402 Wall Street
P.O. Box 984
Key West, FL 33040
Tel: 800/527-8539, 305/294-5988
Fax: 305/294-7806

Jacksonville Film and TV Office
128 E. Forsythe Street, Suite 505
Jacksonville, FL 32202
Tel: 904/630-1905
Fax: 904/630-1485

Lee County Film Office
2180 W. 1st Street, Suite 306
P.O. Box 398
Fort Myers, FL 33902
Tel: 800/330-3161, 813/335-2481
Fax: 813/338-3227

Metro Orlando Film and Television Office
200 E. Robinson Street, Suite 600
Orlando, FL 32801
Tel: 407/422-7159
Fax: 407/843-9514

Miami/Dade Office of Film, TV, and Print
111 N.W. 1st Street, Suite 2510
Miami, FL 33128
Tel: 305/375-3288
For Production Guide information:
    305/442-9444
Fax: 305/375-3266

Northwest Florida/Okaloosa Film
    Commission
1170 Martin Luther King Jr. Boulevard,
    #717
P.O. Box 4097
Fort Walton Beach, FL 32549
Tel: 904/651-7374
Fax: 904/651-7378

Ocala/Marion County Film Commission
110 E. Silver Springs Boulevard
Ocala, FL 34470
Tel: 904/629-2757
Fax: 904/629-1581

Palm Beach County Film Liaison Office
1555 Palm Beach Lakes Boulevard, Suite
    204
West Palm Beach, FL 33401
Tel: 407/233-1000
Fax: 407/683-6957

Space Coast Film Commission
Brevard County Government Center
2725 St. Johns
Melbourne, FL 32940
Tel: 800/93-OCEAN, 407/633-2110
Fax: 407/633-2112

Volusia County Film Office
123 E. Orange Avenue
P.O. Box 910
Daytona Beach, FL 32114
Tel: 800/544-0415, 904/255-0415
Fax: 904/255-5478

Georgia

Georgia Film and Videotape Office
285 Peachtree Center Avenue, Suite 1000
Atlanta, GA 30303
Tel: 404/656-3591
Fax: 404/651-9063

Savannah Film Commission
c/o City Manager's Office
P.O. Box 1027
Savannah, GA 31402
Tel: 912/651-3696
Fax: 912/238-0872

Hawaii

Big Island Film Office
25 Aupuni Street, #219
Hilo, HI 96720
Tel: 808/961-8366
Fax: 808/935-1205

Hawaii Film Office
P.O. Box 2359
Honolulu, HI 96804
Tel: 808/586-2570
Fax: 808/586-2572

Kauai Film Commission
4280-B Rice Street
Lihue, HI 96766
Tel: 808/241-6390
Fax: 808/241-6399

Maui Film Office
200 S. High Street
Wailuku, HI 96793
Tel: 808/243-7710, 808/243-7415
Fax: 808/243-7995

Oahu Film Office
530 S. King Street, #306
Honolulu, HI 96813
Tel: 808/527-6108
Fax: 808/523-4666

Idaho

Idaho Film Bureau
700 W. State Street, 2nd Floor
Boise, ID 83702-0093
Tel: 800/942-8338, 208/334-2470
Fax: 208/334-2631

Illinois

Chicago Film Office
1 N. LaSalle, Suite 2165
Chicago, IL 60602
Tel: 312/744-6415
Fax: 312/744-1378

Illinois Film Office
100 W. Randolph, Suite 3-400
Chicago, IL 60601
Tel: 312/814-3600
Fax: 312/814-6175

Quad Cities Development Group/Film
 Coalition
1830 2nd Avenue, Suite 200
Rock Island, IL 61201
Tel: 309/326-1005
Fax: 309/788-4964

Indiana
Indiana Film Commission
1 North Capitol, #700
Indianapolis, IN 46204-2288
Tel: 317/232-8829
Fax: 317/233-6887

Iowa
Cedar Rapids Area Film Commission
119 1st Avenue S.E.
P.O. Box 5339
Cedar Rapids, IA 52406-5339
Tel: 800/735-5557, 319/398-5009
Fax: 319/398-5089

Greater Des Moines Film Commission
601 Locust Street, Suite 222
Des Moines, IA 50309
Tel: 800/451-2625, 515/286-4960
Fax: 515/244-9757

Iowa Film Office
200 E. Grand Avenue
Des Moines, IA 50309
Tel: 515/242-4726
Fax: 515/242-4859

Kansas
Kansas Film Commission
700 S.W. Harrison Street, Suite 1300
Topeka, KS 66603
Tel: 913/296-4927
Fax: 913/296-6988

Kansas III Film Commission
Lawrence Convention and Visitors Bureau
734 Vermont
Lawrence, KS 66044
Tel: 913/865-4411
Fax: 913/865-4400

Manhattan Film Commission
555 Poyntz, Suite 290
Manhattan, KS 66502
Tel: 913/776-8829

Wichita Convention and Visitors Bureau
100 S. Main, Suite 100
Wichita, KS 67202
Tel: 316/265-2800
Fax: 316/265-0162

Kentucky

Kentucky Film Commission

500 Mero Street, 2200 Capitol Plaza
    Tower

Frankfort, KY 40601

Tel: 800/345-6591, 502/564-3456

Fax: 502/564-7588

Louisiana

Jeff Davis Parish Film Commission

P.O. Box 1207

Jennings, LA 70546-1207

Tel: 318/821-5534

Fax: 318/821-5536

Louisiana Film Commission

P.O. Box 44320

Baton Rouge, LA 70804-4320

Tel: 504/342-8150

Fax: 504/342-7988

New Orleans Film and Video Commission

1515 Poydras Street, Suite 1200

New Orleans, LA 70112

Tel: 504/565-8104

Fax: 504/565-8108

Shreveport-Bossier Film Commission

P.O. Box 1761

Shreveport, LA 71166

Tel: 800/551-8682, 318/222-9391

Fax: 318/222-0056

Maine

The Maine Film Office

59 State House Station

Augusta, ME 04333

Tel: 207/287-5703

Fax: 207/287-8070

Maryland

Maryland Film Commission

601 N. Howard Street

Baltimore, MD 21201-4582

Tel: 800/333-6632, 410/333-6633

Fax: 410/333-0044

Massachusetts

Boston Film Office

Boston City Hall, #716

Boston, MA 02201

Tel: 617/635-3245

Fax: 617/635-3031

Massachusetts Film Office

10 Park Plaza, Suite 2310

Boston, MA 02116

Tel: 617/973-8800

Fax: 617/973-8810

Michigan

Mayor's Office for Film and Television

1126 City-County Building

Detroit, MI 48226

Tel: 313/224-3430

Fax: 313/224-4128

Michigan Film Office
525 W. Ottawa
P.O. Box 30004
Lansing, MI 48933
Tel: 800/477-3456, 517/373-0638
Fax: 517/373-3872

Minnesota
Minnesota Film Board
401 N. 3rd Street, Suite 460
Minneapolis, MN 55401
Tel: 612/332-6493
Fax: 612/332-3735

Mississippi
Columbus Film Commission
P.O. Box 789
Columbus, MS 39703
Tel: 800/327-2686, 601/329-1191
Fax: 601/329-8969

Mississippi Film Office
Box 849
Jackson, MS 39205
Tel: 601/359-3297
Fax: 601/359-5757

Mississippi Gulf Coast Film Office
P.O. Box 569
Gulfport, MS 39502
Tel: 601/863-3807
Fax: 601/863-4555

Natchez Film Commission
422 Main
P.O. Box 1485
Natchez, MS 39121
Tel: 800/647-6724, 601/446-6345
Fax: 601/442-0814

Oxford Film Commission
P.O. Box 965
Oxford, MS 38655
Tel: 601/234-4680
Fax: 60/-234-4655

Tupelo Film Commission
P.O. Box 1485
Tupelo, MS 38802-1485
Tel: 800/533-0611, 601/841-6454
Fax: 601/841-6558

Vicksburg Film Commission
P.O. Box 110
Vicksburg, MS 39180
Tel: 800/221-3536, 601/636-9421
Fax: 601/636-9475

Missouri
Kansas City, Missouri Film Office
10 Petticoat Lane, Suite 250
Kansas City, MO 64106
Tel: 816/221-0636
Fax: 816/221-0189

187

Missouri Film Office
301 West High, #720
P.O. Box 118
Jefferson City, MO 65101
Tel: 573/751-9050
Fax: 573/751-7384

St. Louis Film Office
330 N. 15th Street
St. Louis, MO 63103
Tel: 314/622-3400, ext. 409
Fax: 314/421-2489

Montana
Great Falls Regonal Film Liaison
815 2nd Street South, P.O. Box 2127
Great Falls, MT 59403
Tel: 800/735-8535
Fax: 406/761-6129

Montana Film Office
1424 9th Avenue
Helena, MT 59601
Tel: 800/553-4563, 406/444-2654
Fax: 406/444-1800

Nebraska
Nebraska Film Office
700 S. 16th Street
Lincoln, NE 68508
Tel: 800/228-4307, 402/471-3680
Fax: 402/471-3026

Omaha Film Commission
6800 Mercy Road, Suite 202
Omaha, NE 68106-2627
Tel: 402/444-7736, 402/444-7737
Fax: 402/444-4511

Nevada
Motion Picture Division/Commission on
   Economic Development
555 E. Washington, Suite 5400
Las Vegas, NV 89701
Tel: 800/336-1600, 775/687-4325

Motion Picture Division/Commission on
   Economic Development
5151 S. Carson Street
Carson City, NV 89710
Tel: 800/336-1600, 702/687-4325
Fax: 702/687-445

New Hampshire
New Hampshire Film and TV Bureau
172 Pembroke Road
P.O. Box 1856
Concord, NH 03302-1856
Tel: 603/271-2598
Fax: 603/271-2629

New Jersey

New Jersey Motion Picture/TV
  Commission
153 Halsey Street
P.O. Box 47023
Newark, NJ 07101
Tel: 201/648-6279
Fax: 201/648-7350

New Mexico

Albuquerque TV and Film Commission
P.O. Box 26866
Albuquerque, NM 87125-6866
Tel: 505/842-9918
Fax: 505/247-9101

Las Cruces Film Commission
311 N. Downtown Mall
Las Cruces, NM 88001
Tel: 505/524-8521
Fax: 505/524-8191

Los Alamos County Film Office
P.O. Box 460
Los Alamos, NM 87544-0460
Tel: 505/662-8105
Fax: 505/662-8399

New Mexico Film Office
1100 S. St. Francis Drive
Santa Fe, NM 87504
Tel: 505/827-9810, 800/545-9871
Fax: 505/827-9799

New York

Greater Buffalo Convention and Visitors
  Bureau
107 Delaware Avenue
Buffalo, NY 14202-2801
Tel: 800/283-3256, 716/852-0511,
  ext. 267
Fax: 716/852-0131

Hudson Valley Film and Video Office, Inc.
40 Garden Street, 2nd Floor
Poughkeepsie, NY 12601
Tel: 914/473-0318
Fax: 914/473-0082

New York City Mayor's Office of Film,
  Theatre, and Broadcasting
1697 Broadway, 6th Floor
New York, NY 10019
Tel: 212/489-6710
Fax: 212/307-6237

New York State Governor's Office/Motion
  Picture-TV Development
Pier 62 W. 23rd Street at Hudson River,
  #307
New York, NY 10011
Tel: 212/929-0240
Fax: 212/929-0506

Rochester/Finger Lakes Film/Video Office
126 Andrews Street
Rochester, NY 14604-1102
Tel: 716/546-5490
Fax: 716/232-4822

North Carolina
Durham Convention and Visitors Bureau
101 E. Morgan Street
Durham, NC 27701
Tel: 800/446-8604, 919/687-0288
Fax: 919/683-9555

Greater Wilmington Film Office
1 Estell Lee Place
Wilmington, NC 28401
Tel: 910/762-2611
Fax: 910/762-9765

North Carolina Film Office
430 N. Salisbury Street
Raleigh, NC 27611
Tel: 800/232-9227, 919/733-9900
Fax: 919/715-0151

Western North Carolina Film Commission
P.O. Box 1258
Arden, NC 28704
or: Description of Service/Product:
3 General Aviation Drive, Fletcher, NC
  28732
Tel: 704/687-7234
Fax: 704/687-7552

Winston-Salem Piedmont Triad Film
  Commission
601 W. 4th Street
Winston-Salem, NC 27102
Tel: 910/777-3787 ext. 1237
Fax: 910/721-2209
E-mail: *wsflmoff@aol.com*

North Dakota
North Dakota Film Commission
604 East Boulevard, 2nd Floor
Bismarck, ND 58505
Tel: 800/328-2871, 701/328-2874,
  701/328-2525
Fax: 701/328-4878

Ohio
Greater Cincinnati Film Commission
632 Vine Street, #1010
Cincinnati, OH 45202
Tel: 513/784-1744
Fax: 513/768-8963

Greater Dayton Film Commission
448 Red Haw Road
Dayton, OH 65405
Tel: 513/277-8090
Fax: 513/277-8090

Ohio Film Commission
77 S. High Street, 29th Floor
P.O. Box 1001
Columbus, OH 43266-0413
Tel: 800/848-1300, 614/466-2284
Fax: 614/466-6744

Oklahoma
Oklahoma Film Office
440 S. Houston, Suite 4
Tulsa, OK 74127-8945
Tel: 800/766-3456, 918/581-2660
Fax: 918/581-2244

Oregon
Oregon Film and Video Office
121 S.W. Salmon Street, Suite 300
Portland, OR 97204
Tel: 503/229-5832
Fax: 503/229-6869

Pennsylvania
Pennsylvania Film Bureau
Forum Building, #449
Harrisburg, PA 17120
Tel: 717/783-3456
Fax: 717/234-4560

Pittsburgh Film Office
Benedum Trees Building, Suite 1300
Pittsburgh, PA 15222
Tel: 412/261-2744
Fax: 412/471-7317

Greater Philadelphia Film Office
1600 Arch Street, 12th Floor
Philadelphia, PA 19103
Tel: 215/686-2668
Fax: 215/686-3659

Puerto Rico
Puerto Rico Film Commission
355 F.D. Roosevelt Avenue, Fomento
    Building #106
San Juan, PR 00918
Tel: 809/758-4747
Fax: 809/756-5706

South Carolina
South Carolina Film Office
P.O. Box 7367
Columbia, SC 29202
Tel: 803/737-0490
Fax: 803/737-3104

Upstate South Carolina Film and Video
    Association
P.O. Box 10048
Greenville, SC 29603
Tel: 803/239-3712
Fax: 803/282-8549

South Dakota

Badlands Film Commission
P.O. Box 58
Kadoka, SD 57543-0058
Tel: 800/467-9217, 605/837-2229
Fax: 605/837-2161

South Dakota Film Commission
711 E. Wells Avenue
Pierre, SD 57501-3369
Tel: 800/952-3625, 605/773-3301
Fax: 605/773-3256

Tennessee

Memphis/Shelby County Film Commission
Beale Street Landing
245 Wagner Place #4
Memphis, TN 38103-3815
Tel: 901/527-8300
Fax: 901/527-8326

Nashville Film Office
161 4th Avenue N.
Nashville, TN 37219
Tel: 615/259-4777
Fax: 615/256-3074

Tennessee Film/Entertainment/Music
   Commission
320 6th Avenue N., 7th Floor
Nashville, TN 37243-0790
Tel: 800/251-8594, 615/741-3456
Fax: 615/741-5829

Texas

Amarillo Film Office
1000 S. Polk Street
Amarillo, TX 79101
Tel: 800/692-1338, 806/374-1497
Fax: 806/373-3909

City of Austin
P.O. Box 1088
Austin, TX 78767
Tel: 512/499-2404
Fax: 512/499-6385

Dallas/Fort Worth Regional Film
   Commission
P.O. Box 610246
DFW Airport, TX 75261
Tel: 800/234-5699, 214/621-0400
Fax: 214/929-0916

El Paso Film Commission
1 Civic Center Plaza
El Paso, TX 79901
Tel: 800/351-6024, 915/534-0698
Fax: 915/534-0686

Houston Film Commission
801 Congress
Houston, TX 77002
Tel: 800/365-7575, 713/227-3100
Fax: 713/223-3816

Irving, Texas Film Commission
6309 N. O'Connor Road, Suite 222
Irving, TX 75039-3510
Tel: 800/2-IRVING, 214-/69-0303
Fax: 214/869-4609

San Antonio Film Commission
P.O. Box 2277
San Antonio, TX 78230
Tel: 800/447-3372, 210/207-6700
Fax: 210/270-8782

Texas Film Commission
P.O. Box 13246
Austin, TX 78711
Tel: 512/463-9200
Fax: 512/463-4114

U.S. Virgin Islands

U.S. Virgin Islands Film Promotion Office
P.O. Box 6400
St. Thomas, VI 00804, U.S.V.I.
Tel: 809/775-1444, 809/774-8784
Fax: 809/774-4390

Utah

Central Utah Film Commission
51 S. University Avenue, Suite 110
Provo, UT 84601
Tel: 800/222-8824, 801/370-8390
Fax: 801/370-8050

Color Country Film Commission
906 N. 1400 West Street
George, UT 84770
Tel: 800/233-8824, 801/628-4171
Fax: 801/673-3540

Kanab/Kane County Film Commission
41 S. 100 East
Kanab, UT 84741
Tel: 800/SEE-KANE, 801/644-5033
Fax: 801/644-5923

Moab to Monument Valley Film
    Commission
50 East Center, #1
Moab, UT 84532
Tel: 801/259-6388, 801/587-3235
Fax: 801/259-6399

Park City Film Commission
P.O. Box 1630
Park City, UT 84060
Tel: 800/453-1360, 801/649-6100
Fax: 801/649-4132

Utah Film Commission
324 S. State, Suite 500
Salt Lake City, UT 84114-7330
Tel: 800/453-8824, 801/538-8740
Fax: 801/538-8886

193

Virginia

Metro Richmond Convention and Visitors
    Bureau and Film Office
550 E. Marshall Street
Richmond, VA 23219
Tel: 800/365-7272, 804/782-2777
Fax: 804/780-2577

Virginia Film Office
901 E. Byrd Street, 19th Floor
P.O. Box 798
Richmond, VA 23206-0798
Tel: 804/371-8204
Fax: 804/371-8177

Washington

Tacoma-Pierce County Film Office
906 Broadway
P.O. Box 1754
Tacoma, WA 98401-1754
Tel: 206/627-2836
Fax: 206/627-8783

Washington State Film and Video Office
2001 6th Avenue, Suite 2600
Seattle, WA 98121
Tel: 206/464-7148
Fax: 206/464-7222

West Virginia

West Virginia Film Office
State Capital, Building 6, Room 525
Charleston, WV 25305-0311
Tel: 800/982-3386, 304/558-2234
Fax: 304/558-1189

Wisconsin

City of Milwaukee Film Liaison
809 N. Broadway
Milwaukee, WI 53202
Tel: 414/286-5700
Fax: 414/286-5904

Wisconsin Film Office
123 W. Washington Avenue, 6th Floor
Madison, WI 53702-0001
Tel: 608/267-3456
Fax: 608/266-3403

Wyoming

Wyoming Film Commission
I-25 and College Drive
Cheyenne, WY 82002-0240
Tel: 800/458-6657, 307/777-7777
Fax: 307/777-6904

Jackson Hole Film Commission
P.O. Box E
Jackson, WY 83001
Tel: 307/733-3316
Fax: 307/733-5585

Associations of Film Commissioners

Alabama Film Office
401 Adams Avenue
Montgomery, AL 36104
Tel: 800/248-0033, 334/242-0400
Fax: 334/242-2414

Alaska Film Office
3601 C Street, Suite 700
Anchorage, AK 99503
Tel: 907/269-8137
Fax: 907/269-8136

Albuquerque TV and Film Office
20 First Plaza N.W., Suite 601
Albuquerque, NM 87102
Tel: 505/842-9918, 800/733-9918
Fax: 505/247-9101

Antelope Valley Film Office—Lancaster
44933 North Fern Avenue
Lancaster, CA 93534
Tel: 805/723-6090
Fax: 805/723-5913

Apache Junction Chamber of Commerce
P.O. Box 1747
Apache Junction, AZ 85217-1747
Tel: 602/982-3141
Fax: 602/982-3234

Arizona Film Commission
3800 North Central Avenue, Building D
Phoenix, AZ 85012
Tel: 602/280-1380, 800/523-6695
Fax: 602/280-1384

Arkansas Motion Picture Office
1 State Capital Mall, Room 2C-200
Little Rock, AR 72201
Tel: 501/682-7676
Fax: 501/682-FILM

Bahamas Film and Television Commission
3450 Wilshire Boulevard, Suite 208
Los Angeles, CA 90010
Tel: 213/385-0033
Fax: 213/383-3966

Berkeley CVB/Berkeley Film Office
1834 University Avenue, 1st Floor
Berkeley, CA 94703
Tel: 800/847-4823
Fax: 510/644-2052

Big Bear Lake Film Office
39707 Big Bear Boulevard
P.O. Box 10000
Big Bear Lake, CA 92315
Tel: 909/878-3040
Fax: 909/866-6766

Boulder County Film Commission
P.O. Box 73
Boulder, CO 80306
Tel: 303/442-1044, 800/444-0447
Fax: 303/938-8837

Broward/Ft. Lauderdale Film and
  Television Office
200 East Las Olas Boulevard, Suite #1850
Fort Lauderdale, FL 33301
Tel: 305/524-3113, 800/741-1420
Fax: 305/524-3167

Cedar Rapids Area Film Commission
119 First Avenue S.E.
P.O. Box 5339
Cedar Rapids, IA 52406-5339
Tel: 319/398-5009 ext. 27,
  800/735-5557 ext. 27
Fax: 319/398-5089

Charlotte Region Film Office
112 S. Tryon Street, Suite 1
Charlotte, NC 28284
Tel: 704/347-8942

Charlotte Region Film Office
112 S. Tryon Street, Suite 900
Charlotte, NC 28284
Tel: 800/554-4373, 704/347-8942
Fax: 704/347-8981

Cheyenne Area Film Office
309 W. Lincolnway
Cheyenne, WY 82001
Tel: 307/778-3133, 800/426-5009
Fax: 307/778-3190

Cineaustria
11601 Wilshire Boulevard, Suite 2480
Los Angeles, CA 90025
Tel: 310/477-2038
Fax: 310/477-5141

City of Fillmore Film Commission
524 Sespe Avenue
P.O. Box 487
Fillmore, CA 93016
Tel: 805/524-3701
Fax: 805/524-5707

City of Pasadena
100 North Garfield Avenue, #103
Pasadena, CA 91109
Tel: 818/405-4152
Fax: 818/405-4785

City of Phoenix Film Office
200 West Washington, 10th Floor
Phoenix, AZ 85003-1611
Tel: 602/262-4850
Fax: 602/534-2295

City of Prescott
P.O. Box 2059
Prescott, AZ 86302
Tel: 520/445-3500
Fax: 520/776-6255

City of West Hollywood
8300 Santa Monica Boulevard
West Hollywood, CA 90069-4314
Tel: 213/848-6489
Fax: 310/289-9541

Cochise County Film Commission
1415 W. Melody Lane, Building B
Bisbee, AZ 85603
Tel: 520/432-9454, 520/432-9200
Fax: 520/432-5016

Colorado Motion Picture and TV
    Commission
1625 Broadway, Suite #1700
Denver, CO 80202
Tel: 303/620-4500
Fax: 303/620-4545

Delaware Film Office
99 Kings Highway
P.O. Box 1401
Dover, DE 19903
Tel: 302/739-4271, 800/441-8846
Fax: 302/739-5749

El Dorado/Tahoe Film Commission
542 Main Street
Placerville, CA 95667
Tel: 916/626-4400, 800/457-6279
Fax: 916/642-1624

El Paso Film Commission
1 Civic Center Plaza
El Paso, TX 79901
Tel: 915/534-0698, 800/351-6024
Fax: 915/534-0686

Entertainment Industry Development
    Corporation
6922 Hollywood Boulevard, Suite #606
Los Angeles, CA 90028
Tel: 213/957-1000 ext. 3
Fax: 213/463-0613

Eureka-Humboldt County CVB
1034 Second Street
Eureka, CA 95501-0541
Tel: 707/443-5097, 800/346-3482
Fax: 707/443-5115

Florida Entertainment Commission
505 17th Street
Miami Beach, FL 33139
Tel: 800/716-7770, 305/673-7468
Fax: 305/673-7168

Florida Keys and Key West Film
   Commission
402 Wall Street
P.O. Box 984
Key West, FL 33040
Tel: 305/294-5988, 800/527-8539,
   800/Film Keys
Fax: 305/294-7806

Fresno Convention and Visitors Bureau
808 M Street
Fresno, CA 93721
Tel: 800/788-0836, 209/233-0836
Fax: 209/445-0122

Ghana Film Commission
8306 Wilshire Boulevard, #330
Beverly Hills, CA 90211
Tel: 213/464-8343
Fax: 213/852-4926

Globe Miami Film Commission
1360 North Broad Street
U.S. 60, P.O. Box 2539
Globe, AZ 85502
Tel: 520/425-4495, 800/804-5623
Fax: 520/425-3410

Greater Philadelphia Film Office
1600 Arch Street, 12th Floor
Philadelphia, PA 19103
Tel: 215/686-2668
Fax: 215/686-3659

Greeley/Weld County Film Commission
902 7th Avenue
Greeley, CO 80631
Tel: 970/352-3566
Fax: 970/352-3572

Greenwood Convention and Visitors
   Bureau
P.O. Drawer 739
Greenwood, MS 38935-0739
Tel: 601/453-9197, 800/748-9064
Fax: 601/453-5526

Hong Kong Tourist Association
10940 Wilshire Boulevard, Suite 1220
Los Angeles, CA 90024
Tel: 310/208-2678
Fax: 310/208-1869

Hudson Valley Film and Video Office, Inc.
40 Garden Street, 2nd Floor
Poughkeepsie, NY 12601
Tel: 914/473-0318
Fax: 914/473-0082

Idaho Film Bureau
700 West State Street, Box 83720
Boise, ID 83720-0093
Tel: 208/334-2470, 800/942-8338
Fax: 208/334-2631

Imperial County Film Commission
940 West Main Street, Suite 208
El Centro, CA 92243
Tel: 619/339-4290, 800/345-6437
Fax: 619/352-7876

Iowa Film Office
200 East Grand Avenue
Des Moines, IA 50309
Tel: 515/242-4726
Fax: 515/242-4859

Jacksonville Film and TV Office
128 East Forsythe Street, Suite 505
Jacksonville, FL 32202
Tel: 904/630-1905
Fax: 904/630-1485

Jeff Davis Parish Film Commission
P.O. Box 1207
Jennings, LA 70546-1207
Tel: 318/821-5534
Fax: 318/821-5536

Kansas Film Commission
700 S.W. Harrison Street, Suite 1300
Topeka, KS 66603
Tel: 913/296-4927
Fax: 913/296-6988

Kansas III Film Commission/Lawrence
 CVB
734 Vermont
Lawrence, KS 66044
Tel: 913/865-4411
Fax: 913/865-4400

Kauai Film Commission
4280-B Rice Street
Lihue, HI 96766
Tel: 808/241-6390
Fax: 808/241-6399

Kern County Board of Trade
2101 Oak Street
P. O. Bin 1312
Bakersfield, CA 93302
Tel: 800/500-KERN
Fax: 661/861-2017

Las Cruces Film Commission
311 North Downtown Mall
Las Cruces, NM 88001
Tel: 505/524-8521
Fax: 505/524-8191

Long Beach Office of Special Events
333 W. Ocean Boulevard, 13th Floor
Long Beach, CA 90802
Tel: 310/570-5333
Fax: 310/570-5335

Louisiana Film Commission
P.O. Box 44320
Baton Rouge, LA 70804-4320
Tel: 504/342-8150
Fax: 504/342-7988

Mammoth Location Services
1 Minaret Road
P. O. Box 24
Mammoth Lakes, CA 93546
Tel: 619/934-0628, 800/228-4947
Fax: 619-934-0700

Maryland Film Office
217 E. Redwood Street, 9th Floor
Baltimore, MD 21202
Tel: 410/767-6340, 800/333-6632,
    410/767-0067
Fax: 410/333-0044

Mayor's Office of Art, Culture, and Film
280 14th Street
Denver, CO 80202
Tel: 303/640-2686
Fax: 303/640-2737

Memphis and Shelby City Film, Tape,
    and Music
Beale Street Landing/245 Wagner Place #4
Memphis, TN 38103-3815
Tel: 901/527-8300
Fax: 901/527-8326

Minneapolis Office of
    Film/Video/Recording
323M City Hall – 350 S. 5th Street
Minneapolis, MN 55415
Tel: 612/673-2947
Pager: 612/818-1221
Fax: 612/673-2011

Minnesota Film Board
401 North 3rd Street, Suite 460
Minneapolis, MN 55401
Tel: 612/332-6493
Fax: 612/332-3735

Missouri Film Office
301 West High, #720
P.O. Box 118
Jefferson City, MO 65101
Tel: 573/751-9050
Fax: 573/751-7385

Mobile Film Office
150 South Royal Street
Mobile, AL 36602
Tel: 334/434-7304
Fax: 334/434-7659

Montana Film Office
1424 9th Avenue
Helena, MT 59620
Tel: 406/444-3762, 800/553-4563
Fax: 406/444-4191

Monterey County Film Commission
801 Lighthouse Avenue
P.O. Box 111
Monterey, CA 93942-0111
Tel: 408/646-0910
Fax: 408/655-9244

Motion Picture Division/C.E.D.
555 East Washington, Suite 5400
Las Vegas, NV 89101
Tel: 702/486-2711
Fax: 702/486-2712

Nashville Film Office
161 Fourth Avenue North
Nashville, TN 37219
Tel: 615/259-4777
Fax: 615/256-3074

Natchez Film Commission
422 Main
P.O. Box 1485
Natchez, MS 39121
Tel: 601/446-6345, 800/647-6724
Fax: 601/442-0814

Nebraska Film Office
700 South 16th Street
Lincoln, NE 68509-4666
Tel: 402/471-3680, 800/228-4307
Fax: 402/471-3026

New Jersey Motion Picture/TV
Commission
153 Halsey Street
P.O. Box 47023
Newark, NJ 07101
Tel: 201/648-6279
Fax: 201/648-7350

New Mexico Film Office
1100 South St. Francis Drive
Santa Fe, NM 87504-5003
Tel: 800/545-9871, 545/827-9810
Fax: 505/827-9799

New Orleans Film and Video Commission
1515 Poydras Street, Suite 1200
New Orleans, LA 70112
Tel: 504/565-8104
Fax: 504/565-8108

New York City Mayor's Office of
Film/Theatre/Broadcast
1697 Broadway, #602
New York, NY 10019
Tel: 212/489-6710
Fax: 212/307-6237

New York State Governor's Office/
MP-TV Dev.
633 Third Avenue, 33rd Floor
New York, NY 10017
Tel: 212/803-2330
Fax: 212/803-2339

North Carolina Film Office
430 North Salisbury Street
Raleigh, NC 27611
Tel: 919/733-9900, 800/232-9227
Fax: 919/715-0151

Northwest Florida/Okaloosa Film
  Commission
1170 Martin Luther King Jr. Boulevard,
  #717
P.O. Box 4097
Ft. Walton Beach, FL 32549
Tel: 800/322-3319
Fax: 904/651-7149

Omaha Film Commission
6800 Mercy Road, Suite 202
Omaha, NE 68106-2627
Tel: 402/444-7736, 402/444-7737
Fax: 402/444-4511

Orange County Film Commission
2 Park Plaza, Suite 100
Irvine, CA 92614
Tel: 714/476-2242, 800/628-8033
Fax: 714/476-0513

Page-Lake Powell Film Commission
P.O. Box 727
Page, AZ 86040
Tel: 520/645-2741
Fax: 520/645-3181

Palm Beach City Film and Television
  Commission
1555 Palm Beach Lakes Boulevard, Suite
  414
West Palm Beach, FL 33401
Tel: 561/233-1000, 800/745-FILM
Fax: 561/683-6957

Palm Springs Desert Resorts CVB/
  Film Office
69-930 Highway 111, Suite 201
Rancho Mirage, CA 92270
Tel: 619/770-9000, 800/96-RESORTS
Fax: 619/770-9001

Providence Film Commission
400 Westminster Street, 6th Floor
Providence, RI 02903
Tel: 401/273-3456
Fax: 401/274-8240

Redding Convention and Visitors Bureau
777 Auditorium Drive
Redding, CA 96001
Tel: 530/225-4100, 800/874-7562
Fax: 530/225-4354

Ridgecrest Film Commission
100 West California Avenue
Ridgecrest, CA 93555
Tel: 619/375-8202, 800/847-4830
Fax: 619/371-1654

Rochester/Finger Lakes Film/Video Office
126 Andrews Street
Rochester, NY 14604-1102
Tel: 716/546-5490
Fax: 716/232-4822

Sacramento Area Film Commission
1421 K Street
Sacramento, CA 95814
Tel: 916/264-7777
Fax: 916/264-7788

San Diego Film Commission
402 West Broadway, Suite 1000
San Diego, CA 92101-3585
Tel: 619/234-3456
Fax: 619/234-0571

San Jose Film and Video Commission
333 West San Carlos, Suite #1000
San Jose, CA 95110
Tel: 408/295-9600, 800/726-5673
Fax: 408/295-3937

Scottsdale Film Office
3939 Civic Center Boulevard
Scottsdale, AZ 85251
Tel: 602/994-2636
Fax: 602/994-7780

Seattle / Mayor's Office of Film and Video
600 4th Avenue, 2nd Floor
Seattle, WA 98104
Tel: 206/684-5030
Fax: 206/684-5360

Sedona Film Commission
P.O. Box 2489
Sedona, AZ 86339
Tel: 520/204-1123
Fax: 520/204-1064

Shreveport-Bossier Film Commission
P.O. Box 1761
Shreveport, LA 71166
Tel: 318/222-9391, 800/551-8682
Fax: 318/222-0056

Sonoma County Film Liaison Office
5000 Roberts Lake Road, Suite A
Rohnert Park, CA 94928
Tel: 707/586-8100, 707/586-8110
Fax: 707/586-8111

South Dakota Film Commission
711 East Wells Avenue
Pierre, SD 57501-3369
Tel: 605/773-3301
Fax: 605/773-3256

Southeastern Connecticut Film Office
P.O. Box 89
New London, CT 06320-4974
Tel: 800/657-FILM, 860/444-2206
Fax: 860/442-4257

Space Coast Film Commission
c/o Brevard County Government Center
2725 St. Johns
Melbourne, FL 32940
Tel: 407/633-2110, 800/93-OCEAN
Fax: 407/633-2112

Temecula Valley Film Council
P. O. Box 1786
Temecula, CA 92593
Tel: 909/699-6267
Fax: 909/694-1999

Tennessee Film/Entertainment/Music
   Commission
320 6th Avenue North, 7th Floor
Nashville, TN 37243-0790
Tel: 615/741-3456, 800/251-8594
Fax: 615/741-5829

The Inland Empire Film Commission
301 E. Vanderbilt Way, Suite 100
San Bernardino, CA 92408
Tel: 909/890-1090, 800/500-4367
Fax: 909/890-1088

The Maine Film Office
59 State House Station
Augusta, ME 04333-0059
Tel: 207/287-5703
Fax: 207/287-8070

Tupelo Film Commission
P.O. Box 1485
Tupelo, MS 38802-1485
Tel: 601/841-6454, 800/533-0611
Fax: 601/841-6558

Utah Film Commission
324 South State, Suite 500
Salt Lake City, UT 84114-7330
Tel: 801/538-8740, 800/453-8824
Fax: 801/538-8886

Utah's Southwest Film Commission
906 N. 1400 West
St. George, UT 84770
Tel: 801/628-4171, 800/233-8824
Fax: 801/673-3540

Vallejo/Solano County Film Commission
495 Mare Island Way
Vallejo, CA 94590
Tel: 707/642-3653, 800/4-VALLEJO
Fax: 707/644-2206

Volusia County Film Office
123 E. Orange Avenue
P.O. Box 910
Daytona Beach, FL 32114
Tel: 904/255-0415, 800/544-0415
Fax: 904/255-5478

Washington State Film and Video Office
2001 6th Avenue, Suite 2600
Seattle, WA 98121
Tel: 206/464-7148
Fax: 206/464-7222

West Virginia Film Office
State Capital, Building 6, Room 525
Charleston, WV 25305-0311
Tel: 304/558-2234, 800/982-3386
Fax: 304/558-1189

Western North Carolina Film Commission
P.O. Box 1258
Arden, NC 28704
Tel: 704/687-7234
Fax: 704/687-7552

Wickenburg Film Commission
216 North Frontier Street
P.O. Drawer CC
Wickenburg, AZ 85358
Tel: 520/684-5479
Fax: 520/684-5470

Winston-Salem Piedmont Triad Film
    Commission
601 West Fourth Street
Winston-Salem, NC 27102
Tel: 910/777-3787 ext. 1237
Fax: 910/721-2209

Wyoming Film Office
I-25 and College Drive
Cheyenne, WY 82002-0240
Tel: 307/777-7777, 800/458-3372
Fax: 307/777-6904

Yampa Valley Film Board, Inc.
Box 772305
Steamboat Springs, CO 80477
Tel: 970/879-0882
Fax: 970/879-2543

Index

Books from Allworth Press

Producing for Hollywood: How to Succeed as an Independent Producer for Movies and Television
by Paul Mason and Donald L. Gold (softcover, 6 × 9, 256 pages, $19.95)

The Health and Safety Guide for Film, TV, and Theater
by Monona Rossol (softcover, 6 × 9, 256 pages, $19.95)

The Screenwriter's Legal Guide, Second Edition
by Stephen F. Breimer (softcover, 6 × 9, 320 pages, $19.95)

Selling Scripts to Hollywood
by Katherine Atwell Herbert (softcover, 6 × 9, 176 pages, $12.95)

Writing Television Comedy
by Jerry Rannow (softcover, 6 × 9, 224 pages, $14.95)

So, You Want to Be a Screenwriter: How to Face the Fears and Take the Risks
by Sara Caldwell and Marie-Eve Kielson (softcover, 6 × 9, 224 pages, $14.95)

Writing Scripts Hollywood Will Love: An Insider's Guide to Film and Television Scripts that Sell, Revised Edition
by Katherine Atwell Herbert (softcover, 6 × 9, 160 pages, $12.95)

Clues to Acting Shakespeare
by Wesley Van Tassel (softcover, 6 × 9, 208 pages, $16.95)

An Actor's Guide—Your First Year in Hollywood
by Michael Saint Nicholas (softcover, 6 × 9, 256 pages, $16.95)

Promoting Your Acting Career
by Glenn Alterman (softcover, 6 × 9, 224 pages, $18.95)

Creating Your Own Monologue
by Glenn Alterman (softcover, 6 × 9, 192 pages, $14.95)

Technical Theater for Nontechnical People
by Drew Campbell (softcover, 6 × 9, 256 pages, $18.95)

Artists Communities: A Directory of Residencies in the United States That Offer Time and Space for Creativity, Second Edition
by the Alliance of Artists' Communities (softcover, 6¾ × 10, 256 pages, $18.95)

Please write to request our free catalog. To order by credit card, call 1-800-491-2808 or send a check or money order to Allworth Press, 10 East 23rd Street, Suite 510, New York, NY 10010. Include $5 for shipping and handling for the first book ordered and $1 for each additional book. Ten dollars plus $1 for each additional book if ordering from Canada. New York State residents must add sales tax.

To see our complete catalog on the World Wide Web, or to order online, you can find us at *www.allworth.com*.